MYSTERY OF THE AGES

Christ in You the Hope of Glory

Dr. J. Paul Lambert

Originally written by Dr. J. Paul Lambert in 1959
Supplemental material is submitted by Tim Adrian.
Church bundle orders (minimum of ten): tim@wbc-hutch.org

Shirt-Tale Publications; Hutchinson, Kansas
ISBN-10: 1539396371
ISBN-13: 9781539396376

DEDICATION

To my wife, Emily Ruth Kite Lambert, this work is affectionately dedicated. For her love, faithfulness, and devotion, I praise God, who gave her to be my life's companion.
Appreciation
To my brother, James W. Lambert, whom I hold in high esteem, I owe a debt of gratitude, for assisting in the publishing of this book.
To a great host of friends, whom I cherish highly, who have encouraged the writing of this book, I am most appreciative.
J. Paul Lambert, Evangelist

CONTENTS

PREFACE

Originally written nearly 60 years ago, *Mystery of the Ages* has long been a lost book. After all of these years only a few copies have survived and since it was independently published, there wasn't any chance of having it reprinted. From time to time while speaking publicly, I have dropped my grandpa's name and have been continually amazed that people would approach me with testimony of his ministry. Of course, questions about this book, and its availability would surface as well.

While speaking to a group of missionaries in Brazil, I became acquainted with Joe Flippin. He also gave compliments of my grandfather and after some correspondence converted this work into a digital format. The book you now hold is the newest edition and the first to include some appendix material I found in a box of my grandpa's notes.

This book has only been slightly edited; mostly for lay-out purposes. I wanted to keep the tone, personality and tenor of Dr. Lambert's message as close to the original as possible. It is with great joy we make this work available to you and it is with sincere prayer we trust you will be blessed by it.

May we all know the Mystery, Glory and Power of the Indwelling Christ!

Dr. Tim Adrian

PROLOGUE

One need not expect the usual, the ordinary or the commonplace while in pursuit of this great "mystery," rather, anticipate the extraordinary, the rare, and that which is beyond the usual scope of affairs.

This, then, Dear Reader, is to be a venture, a study, an experience; a heart thrilling and soul satisfying journey through the ages and generations of the past, conducted by our blessed Guide and Teacher, the Holy Spirit.

I speak of the "Mystery of the Ages." According to the Scriptures a "rich mystery" and a "glorious mystery," the unveiling of which, I earnestly pray, will bring you "joy unspeakable," "peace that passeth understanding," and knowledge of "riches and glory untold."

This writer challenges you to have your heart and mind prepared for a soul-shocking impact. We travel in the company of the Paraclete (Holy Spirit) who will bring to bear upon our sensibilities awesome and fearful things, which have come thundering down the stairway of time.

Pray that our Guide and Teacher, the Holy One, will not only reveal these great mysteries, but by these unveiled profound truths He will elevate our lives from the humdrum and commonplace to a place where daily we are thrilled to walk where angels tread. Does not your very heart thrill at the prospect?

Remember this is a mystery!

INTRODUCTION

Satan plots our destruction. He puts up a desperate struggle. Thus we are to go on a strange and hazardous adventure. We shall traverse paths unknown. This is a daring mission for we must visit the realm of the dead.

A neighbor said, "I know all about death, I attended a funeral and viewed the corpse." But silent lips, the motionless form, and stilled frame of dust, can teach us but little of the mystery of death. Earth dwellers cannot see that which is beyond the grave.

Postmortem or a Trip to the Morgue

May we, as Christian reporters, on the trail of a great mystery, take our positions in a corner of the morgue; as the mortician, police surgeon, detectives, laboratory technicians, and coroner bend over the body of one who expired suddenly. This singular examination is not to determine the cause of death, but to investigate death itself.

No speculation, please! The information gleaned is to be revealed to the physically alive earth dwellers. Our findings, based upon proven facts, will be reported to them that they may thus think and act in terms of what is beyond the mortuary, the shroud, the coffin, and the narrow - cold - damp grave.

Will the undertaker's hands be the last to handle us? The eyes that beheld us as the casket lid is closed, will they be the last to look upon us? To the unregenerate this may seem to create an atmosphere of eeriness. But! We must seek desperately to answer these and manifold other questions.

How can we obtain this information? Since the dead are forbidden a return, we must go where they reside. We go beyond the morgue, and the mortician's table, or the grave. We follow the soul of man - we go where it goes.

Postmortem Information

Into this death-room, with its flickering shadows, strides a kindly and serious looking stranger. He holds, in his right hand, the Word of God. Immediately all eyes are upon him as with a demeanor of authority he momentarily fastens his attention upon the deceased.

There is a moment of suspense. Suddenly, a voice startles the onlookers; they hear a strange announcement, "We are to go on a daring adventure - a strange mission. We must visit the realm of the dead." The commanding one continues, "Satan plots our destruction. We must uncover his plot. It must be exposed!"

We are neither to heed man made clattering nonsense nor the honey tongued priests of Beelzebub, the strange one continues. "We are to depart the realm of the living, and proceed to the death-regions by way of the written-Word. Stay close by it, while remembering The Living-Word, The Author of the written-Word, accompanies us," counsels our unique conductor.

Assignment Suicide

Suddenly the room becomes fiercely brilliant! Enormous power rests upon the speaker for now he reads from the Word of God. Immediately we are swept to a point of observance where we survey a maelstrom of violence - orgies of torture. Human souls, who by procrastination had gambled against time, and lost!

These in the mad-house of the universe, their minds disarranged by their own Christ rejecting folly. Hate crazed ghosts - savage beings - tormented by their desire to commit eternal suicide. They know this is but for one night - a night of terror that continues for a limitless eternity. Once these were human beings. Now only characters! Beings unknown! Living dead!

Bad Timing

These Christ rejecters, now hell-converted (too late), once thought they, with curses, could laugh at God's Word - mock His threats and spurn His love. This ordeal without end is self-inflicted!

Eve listened to words. Children of Eve harkens to thoughts. The one who listens to his own mind is doomed. Take heed! Harkin to a sly little secret. Satan tempts by remote control. The mind is his area of operation.

The Body Emptied of All But Death

As death moves into the body, the "I" moves out. One's destination is determined by arrangements made in advance. God's Book supplies all the needed information. One should not postpone the making of these arrangements till death valley nights. The "King of Terrors" may come suddenly. One minute in hell may teach a person all that he refused to learn on earth during an entire life time. That minute may become night forever.

1

THE MYSTERY OF TWO PERSONS IN ONE WHICH IS, "CHRIST IN YOU, THE HOPE OF GLORY"

Remember how stunned you were when you received the message of the passing of a close friend? It seemed impossible, it just could not be, and you saw them only a day or so ago. Certainly then, you may now be stunned, your mind shocked, your reason challenged as you hear the following announcement:

> Dear Christian:
>   You are dead! You passed away! The body of sin has been destroyed! If Christ be in you, then the body is dead. Note the scriptures: For ye are dead, and your life is hid with Christ (Colossians 3:3).
> Yours forever,
> The Apostle Paul

A Profound Secret
I trust your poor feeble heart is not too shocked? But! This is a mystery, something beyond the usual scope of affairs. Let us dedicate ourselves to finding the solution to this profound secret.

Crucifixion Kills

Would you be willing to die? Are you willing to move out of the "body of sin" into Christ, and then allow Him to come down from Heaven and live His life in your body? Should you make such a surrender you could then say with the Apostle Paul, "I am crucified with Christ (crucifixion kills): nevertheless I live; yet not I, but Christ liveth in me: and the life which I now live in the flesh I live by the faith of the Son of God, who loved me, and gave Himself for me" (Galatians 2:20).

Christ in You

Consider the mystery of two persons in one: Both indwelling the same body! How can this be? Could two possibly merge and become one? Nothing like this could ever occur in the realm of the natural. I believe the Apostle Paul not only understood the answer to our mystery clothed query, but his great heart's desire was to reveal the solution, by way of his Spirit-controlled pen.

Unexplored Regions

May the blessed Holy Spirit quicken our spiritual senses, as He also illuminates His own word. May this enlighten a new passageway into unexplored regions of the Christian experience. The spirit-realm, mystery-shrouded as it is, is inaccessible to the carnally minded. "For they that are after the flesh do mind the things of the flesh; but they that are after the Spirit the things of the Spirit" (Romans 5:8).

Soul-Rocking Impact

Christian, is your feeble heart now prepared for a shock, a most pleasurable soul-rocking impact? As the splendor of this powerful and priceless mystery collides with your sensibilities, you may cry out in the words of the Apostle Paul, "Lord, help, lest I should be exalted above measure through the abundance of these revelations!"

Will you, now, take the Scriptures, believe each word, and accept at face value the primary, ordinary and literal meaning of them? Are we not to believe that the Spirit carefully selected the very words He wanted used; knew what He wanted to say and how to say. If the plain sense makes good sense, seek no other sense, lest it become nonsense! Words are the vehicles of thought, one cannot think except in terms of words. Try it!

A Faith Challenging Statement
"If ye then be risen ..." What kind of a person is risen? Why, only the one who first died. The Holy Spirit informs us we are "Risen with Christ, and we are to seek those things which are above, where Christ sitteth on the right hand of God" (Colossians 3:1). "And hath raised us up together, and made us sit together in Heavenly places in Christ Jesus." (Ephesians 2:6). What person can sit in Heavenly places? Why... Only a dead one! "For ye are dead and your life is hid with Christ in God" (Colossians 3:3).

Not for Unbelievers
Unbelief cries, "Too baffling! It is in direct contradiction with my experience. I'm not dead, I still live." Carnality begs, "I am too materially minded. I cannot accept the plain statement of Scripture. It is too shocking - too opposed to my experience - how can I logically believe that I actually died?" Allow me to hear some carnal minded Dr. Dry As Dust or Rev. Tickle Their Ears explain this away by stating, "It is only a beautiful metaphorical figuration," then I can believe it.

He Who Listens to His Own Mind is Doomed
We are not to look into our minds to see what we think. We are not to consult our own experiences to determine if a Bible statement be so. Satan operates in the realm of the mind! Faith unblushingly, and with praise to God says, "I am to believe this portion of God's Holy Word, even as all His Word is to be received, believed, and appropriated. Even though I find a Scriptural teaching which directly contradicts, opposes, or runs counter to my experience, logic, or

judgment; I will still believe and accept at face value the plain, literal Word."

The Mystery of the Written Word
Words are the vehicles of thought. One cannot think except in terms of words. Try it! God spake all these words (Exodus 20:1). The scoffer cries, "Men wrote the Bible!" Yes, I reply, Men wrote the Bible, But! May I hasten to add, God told those men what to write. He gave them the exact words He wanted used. The original Word is in Heaven. An angel noted this fact to Daniel. Man will one day stand before God and face that original. God pity the man who has taken from or added to that word. Woe unto that individual!

The Christian's Death is a Passageway into Unexplored Realms of the Christian Experience
Every new-born Christian is invited of his Savior Guide to accompany Him in the exploration of vast regions of the Spirit-realm. Having "The Mind of Christ" and being of a willing spirit, the believer may be led by his Teacher-Guide through a passageway into unexplored realms of Christian experience. Once we have crossed the boundary line we may see and hear fearful and awesome things.

The Holy Spirit will discover for us seemingly unbelievable facts - facts that become realities as we experience them. Our Creator-Teacher will not only impart information - out of this world information, but also demonstrate, by making real, the fact and reality of the Christian's death (cross-death) and resurrection.

A Mystery – Shrouded Truth
This soul stimulating, mystery-shrouded truth can only be grasped by the one who has surrendered to the "Mind of Christ" (Philippians 2:5). Furthermore, this knowledge can only be ac-

quired as its truth is examined, and as the Holy Spirit demonstrates the power of its reality.

A Hell-Shattering Truth; the Mystery of Two Persons in One

What is the dynamic of this rich and glorious hell-shattering truth? The surrendered believer who explores this dynamic Bible revelation will discover his wonderful Guide is alongside to lead him to a rich uranium deposit of resources of mighty sin destructive power. Draw on the resources here discovered.

Satan laughs at man's puny little carnal weapons. But, his demon powers are sent scampering back into the darkness of Hell's black realm when we start blasting away with the atomic-thrust of the word of His power. The creative power of God's Word can demolish the "Strong-Holds of Satan."

The Mystery of the Living-Word; Making Alive the Written-Word

"It is the Spirit that quickeneth; the flesh profiteth nothing: The words that I speak unto you, they are Spirit, and they are life" (John 6:63). "The word became flesh, and dwelt among us..." (John 1:4). The word living within can make alive the written word. The Living-Word dwelling Himself in the believer can make His Word written truth, even this truth, actually so within the believer.

Remember, this is the mystery of the ages! The Father teaches, "You are dead and risen." By dwelling the "Dead and risen Crucified One" within you, God can say it is so because it then becomes so.

He Brings His Cross-Death into you

Jesus Christ experienced the cross, the tomb, and the resurrection. The dictionary defines, "experience is the actual living through an event." Jesus actually passed through the event called Calvary. He experienced the cross - He experienced the tomb - He experienced the resurrection.

He brings the experience of His cross-death into the body of the believer, by dwelling Himself within. "Christ in you (is) the hope of glory" (Colossians 1:27). The Apostle Paul understood and experienced this soul-tingling truth when he with great exuberance cried, "I am crucified with Christ: nevertheless I live..." There you have both death and resurrection with Christ. Since the written Word says "You are dead and risen" the living word can create the reality of the fact within.

An Atomic Explosion in the Devil's Camp

The atomic-power of our Savior's cross-death - His tomb experience - His resurrection power, are at the disposal of the appropriator. Jesus invaded Satan's death-realm, spoiled principalities and powers - declared Satan a defeated for destroyed the Devil's power of death, and by the dynamite of His resurrection dropped a mighty atomic-like-bomb that left nothing but destruction and ruin in Lucifer's camp.

Sin- Destructive Forces

Now, today, the believer is invited of the glorious conquering Lord, "Stand fast in the power of His might" (Ephesians 6:10). Sin-destructive forces are available and at our disposal. Let us blast away with the atomic-thrust of God's Word at Satan's strongholds and fortresses of sin.

Universe-Creating Power

The Creator of the world is the Author of the word. Since the Author-Teacher- Creator could by the "power of His word" actually speak worlds into existence, could He not also, by the power of that same word, make the written facts become living facts? This is creative power working in you.

Sin Reigns Only unto Death

"That as sin reigned unto death" (Romans 5:21). Sin cannot touch a dead man. Blast Satan with this! Sin can reign only unto death. Here is where unbelievable facts must become a reality. It is God's own plan, in you for Satan's defeat.

The Creator-Savior will create within, the reality of that which God teaches is actually so. This unbelievable fact becomes a reality as we experience it. This is God's "Word-Sword" which He offers for your use against Satan and sin.

The Spirit will demonstrate the fact of your cross-death. He was put to death so sin can have no power over you. You see, sin reigns only unto death! By believing the Creator's statement, we thus give permission for the creation of an inward impression that we are "dead with Him to sin, and risen with Him for righteousness".

"Neither yield ye your members as instruments of unrighteousness unto sin," teaches our Holy God. Many attempt to obey this, but fail utterly. Why? Simply because they do not believe the remainder of this startling verse, which says, "But yield yourselves unto God (the indwelling Christ), as those alive from the dead."

If we obey this verse, then the next one will become a true fact within us "For sin shall not have dominion over you" (Romans 6:7). "For he that is dead is freed from sin." "How shall we that are dead to sin, live any longer therein?" (See Romans 6:2, 7 &13-14) These truths become ours when we, by faith, appropriate them.

Back Through the Tomb to the Old Life of Sin; A Ghoulish Walking-Corpse Existence
"Shall we continue in sin that grace may abound" (Romans 6:1)? To go back into the old sinful life would be much like running back through our death-tomb; donning the old stinking shroud-garment and living a sort of walking corpse existence. The Spirit of Christ is there within you, to detest through your heart the flesh-filthiness and disgustingly dirty obscenities of the past back through the tomb death-life. God forbid! Unthinkable! God rebuke such a hellish, Satan-inspired, foul, rebellious thought! It would be a ghoulish, devil-empowered, resurrection in-reverse sort of life.

Satan sends Demons to Harass, Weary and Exhaust

Oh! I know well enough, after we are saved, Satan dispatches his sin-demons to harass, gore, and defeat. These often gouge and harass to stir up the sins of the flesh. They cause misery oppression, powerlessness, and frustration. Satan's goon squad can do a most wily, deceitful, tricky, and subtle bit of undercover - behind the scenes, skullduggery. By a very clever and powerful ingenious method transmits demon thoughts onto the human mind.

The transmitter of these thoughts follows a well-planned program as he casts these ideas onto the stage of the mind. Evil spirits exercise exceeding great power as they impress these dispatches upon the thinking processes of their victims.

These often appear as temper, pride, hate, jealousy, avarice, worry and lust - causing misery, oppression, frustration, and powerlessness. But! There is a way of victory over all these. The Victor resides within!!! Amen! Praise God! Thanks be to God who gives us the victory through His Son the Lord Jesus (See 1 Corinthians 15:57).

Just believe the written Word when it teaches "For sin shall not have dominion over you. . ." (Romans 6:14a) thus the Living Word (dwelling within) will teach you the written word is so.

The Author-Teacher of the Word

The Author of the holy eternal Word lovingly dwells Himself within. Get to yourself - be alone - there in your prayer closet. Be silent. Listen! See? You find you are never alone. Now, let His calm enter into your being. "Peace – peace I give you." The Author of these words abides within. Listen attentively - softly He whispers. Feel, feel, the Creator's heart, beating gently beating - within your own!

Study, Discussion & Application Points for Chapter 1

1. Read and study this chapter.
2. The key verse for this chapter is Galatians 2:20: *"I am crucified with Christ: nevertheless I live; yet not I, but Christ liveth in me: and*

the life which I now live in the flesh I live by the faith of the Son of God, who loved me, and gave himself for me."

3.   Look up the following passages and read them over several times. Consider each verse, phrase and word. It may prove to be helpful to consult a solid Bible dictionary and/or commentary. Write down the key thoughts that God has given you.
     •   Colossians 3:1-3
     •   Romans 6:3-6:8

4.   Dr. Lambert tells us the Indwelling Christ is our Author-Teacher-Guide as we study the scriptures. Look up the following passages and note the key points:
     •   John 6:63
     •   1 Corinthians 2:10-13

5.   Scoffers and unbelievers may have objections to the truth and authority of Scripture. Look at these passages and note the Bible's own testimony:
     •   2 Peter 1:21
     •   1 Corinthians 2:14-15

6.   Dr. Lambert teaches us to respond to devilish impulses (temptations) by "Blasting Satan with the Truth". Note these verses and write down the key thought:
     •   Colossians 2:12
     •   I Corinthians 15:57
     •   Romans 6:13-14
     •   Titus 2:11-14

2

THE MYSTERY OF ONE PERSON IN THREE

Soul-Body-Spirit

"I pray God your whole spirit and soul and body be preserved blameless unto the coming of our Lord Jesus Christ" (1 Thessalonians 5:23). "What is man that Thou art mindful of Him, and the son of man, that Thou visitest him" (Psalm 8:4)?

Just what is man? The dictionary says he is an "adult male" - while evolution declares he is the final result of one lonely little unmarried amoeba, who, one afternoon, about, oh, 3:15 P.M. got to pucker'n, an pucker'n, and finally - "boom"!!! Just like that, he pucker'd his little fool self clear in two.

Now these super-science E-vol-vo-spoof-us fellers called the East end "Ma" and the West end "Pa." No one, to this very day, knows for sure, who had the honor of uniting this happy little couple in that first matrimonial venture, but! they think it was "The Missing Link." Leastwise he "ain't" showed up since.

After that it was no time at all till a lot of cute lil baby cells were pucker'n and bust'n all over the place. So this is the yarn of that first poor little lonesome, one-cylindered cell which turned out to be the "Grand Pappy" of us all. This Devil-lution "cell" is Satan's own "sell".

Only a fool would surrender his position in Genesis for such poor logic as is offered by modern speculation. What a conglomeration of grotesque absurdities has been whomped up by these Satan-sellers.

The Creator's Hands

The Creator-Savior is, in His omnipotence, sufficiently capable to create first-man by a direct act. He requires no assistance from non-believers who think (?) the Genesis account too miraculous, so, they try to thin it out by spreading it over "millions of years." Thus they would require thousands of redundant, ridiculous, absurd, and in-credible "cracked-head miracles" instead of one credible God per-formed direct act.

One should have no difficulty believing the Creator's own decla-ration, "And the Lord God formed man of the dust of the ground." In fact one should have to believe it. There is a tender suggestion here: although the Creator "spoke", the worlds into existence, He must be-cause of His loving heart, "form" man, His grandest and most pre-cious creation, with His own hands - hands that one day were to be "pierced."

Jesus Christ Performed Creative Acts

One day, while walking this malady ridden earth, the compassion-ate Creator-Savior found an afflicted one who was blind from birth. Immediately, Jesus procured a handful of clay and made spittle of it. Pressing this mud pack into the empty sockets, He commanded the "about-to-be-repaired-man" to wash in the Pool of Salome.

Instantly, as the obedient one washed away the excess clay, sight was received. Oh! Yes, and why not? Had he not just met the One who created man in the first place? The loving Creator found a man who needed a "repair job;" reaching down He scooped up into creative hands, some of the same "stuff" with which He had created man - with it He repaired him.

As easily, and as quickly, as our God created a pair eyes for this blind man, a leg, an arm or hand for others who needed to be made whole or repaired, so with skill and dexterity He, by direct touch, with His own hands, created Adam by "turning dust into flesh." Breathless fact! The one reading this, will one day discover, his flesh has re-turned to dust.

In the words of the poet: "Life is real, life is earnest! And the grave is not its goal. Dust thou art, to dust returneth; Was not spoken of the soul."

What is This Strange Creature Called "I"?

What is man? Is he no more than skin and bones and a hank of hair in his makeup? What is this strange creature called "I", "Me" - "Myself"? Am I just fears, thoughts and sensations, loves, hates, emotions, pains and passions? Who, what is this stranger called "Self"? Is it just my body? Am I no more than a few chemicals, H20, and a breath of air?

Man's Physical Frame: A Composite Thing

Man's body is a composite part; made up of potatoes from Idaho, beef from Texas, bread from Kansas, fruit from California, and "please pass the salt" from Hutchinson. Permit science to assist our interesting investigation of the outward man", with its astonishing assertion that nature has a seven year program which provides a completely rebuilt body every seven years of one's natural life.

Mother Nature, by this ever continuing process, sloughs off the old cells during the course of these seven years; while by the process of eating (I must agree I rather enjoy this latter process) she donates me another body during the same length of time. All this for the price of a grocery bill.

By the time one reaches the age of fifty, he will have dwelt in seven different bodies. Having traded in his last for a later model. Then will then be living in his eighth. Yet all this time he is still the same person!

It is a sort of a daily trade in a bit of the old one, for a bit of the new. But! Who is the "I" that stays right in there (unchanging), while all this trading in going on? I hope I am more than just the food I eat. If that were true, I have come and gone a good many times. I met a friend of mine the other day who apparently, is coming faster than he is going.

Which Body is "I"?

If the "I" is my body, then in a state of perplexity, I hasten to inquire, "Pray tell, which one?" Well, then, is the "I" my brain? If, so, which brain? Surely I rate a new brain with each new out-coming seven-year model! By the way, I don't believe one's teeth are included in the above deal, I think one must pay cash when you order your new ones.

The Apostle Paul must have been musing along this line when he wrote, "Though our outward man perish, yet the inward man is renewed day by day" (2 Corinthians 4:16).

Man, a Living Soul

Man (the "I") is more than particles of chemical dust, atoms, and cells. "The Lord God, formed man of the dust of the ground (physical frame still lifeless, until God touched it with His divine breath) and breathed into his nostrils the breath of life; and man became a living soul."

Man does not have a soul. He is a soul!

Coming forth from the Creator's direct touch, Adam, the first human being, became a living (not a dying) soul. It would, then, hardly be proper to ask, does man have a soul? For, man is a soul! Man has a body. That body is "Fearfully and wonderfully made: marvelous are Thy works; and that my soul knoweth right well" (Psalm 139:14). Perhaps this last refers also to the soul itself. As great as the physical part of man's creation, consider, now, how much even greater is the mystery of the soul.

The Soul a Mystery

Our investigation, thus far, has turned up one surprising fact after another.

King of Terrors

First - the "I" (inward man - Romans 7:22) is more than the body of flesh (outward man - 2 Corinthians 4:16). Man is a soul, but possesses a body; he may dwell within that body as a tenant within a house. He resides there, only as a temporary dweller.

His residence there may be suddenly interrupted by another tenant, the "King of Terrors," who with rasping, wheezing voice will order him, "Off these premises;" off the soul must go, while, "It (death) shall dwell in his tabernacle, because it is none of his" (Job 18:14-15). The Holy Spirit, through the Apostle Paul, calls the body an "earthly house," a tabernacle (temporary abode). The moving out of that house is death (2 Corinthians 5:1).

Will the "I" survive the corpse?

Second - Since self has already survived several "seven year bodies", will he not survive the last one? The man of three score and ten has survived ten bodies; will he not survive his corpse? The soul, or Paul's inward man, will launch out on the Sea of Eternal Adventure – the "I" will have a sudden change of address. "Absent from the body," is Paul's way of putting it (2 Corinthians 5:8).

Loved ones gather about the casket, looking into the cold face, gazing upon those silent lips, they sorrowfully inquire, "Where is she? What is she doing? Does she remember? Does she care?

Earth Dwellers See No Farther Than the Grave

Third - the SOUL is invisible to the natural or physical eye. Here, then, is a deep mystery. I cannot be seen by physical eye, so the Creator must clothe the soul with an earthly substance so that I may be manifested to natural sight.

As a material-man only, am I capable of making a visual impression upon earth dwellers. The dictionary defines the term invisible as something "Not in sight: not presently apparent." According to that, I exist, but am not presently apparent.

More Than a Mud-Ball and a Puff of Air

If the body part of the "I" were dissolved - say reduced to a handful of dust; would you point to that little pile, and say, "There he is?" How naive, to imagine that man is not more than dust and water - a little more than a talking mud-ball with a puff of air. Our God can perform the miracle of turning dust into flesh. The King of Terrors performs the reverse miracle of turning flesh into dust.

The Earthly Material Called Flesh is Nothing More than the Outward Manifestation of the Inward Man

What is this inward man (soul man) who can display himself to earth dwellers, only as he remains in an earth-body? What is the essential essence that underlies the outward manifestation? Is this vital, permanent, fundamental entity only a shadowy vision?

What is this beings in general aspect? Does he have form, substance or structure? Is the frame of the soul of unknown, non-earth, material?

Three Thousand Eight Hundred and Eighteen Years in a Tomb, Yet Still Alive

Let us step aboard the high velocity time-ship "Flight-O-Time" to be transported, with the celerity of light, backwards across thirty-eight centuries to a point in the far distant past known as B.C. 1857. Here we find Abraham in his deathbed; "Then Abraham gave up the ghost (soul), and died in a good old age, an old man, and full of years: and was gathered to his people. "

Still Alive

Now! Let us pursue eternity-fretting Old Man Time leisurely wending his way through one thousand eight hundred years of Old Testament history, Eventually, after measuring days- nights - months - and long years, this aged yet never aging Father Time, advances through the lazy-moving centuries, to a time point designated as A. D. 33.

Here we find an astonished multitude who had just heard the Maker of man and eternity, the Lord Jesus Christ, assert that Abraham, Isaac, and Jacob, though dead, lo, those many long centuries, were at that moment, still alive (Matthew 22:32-33).

Reader! Here is a heart-quickening thought, at the moment you read this, they are still alive.

We Walk by Faith, Not by Sight

Should the veil of flesh be removed from our eyes, as it certainly will be at death, we could without doubt, see - actually see by sight (soul eyes), that which we now see (by faith) through our faith eyes.

The indwelling Narrator reveals by the Scriptures the true facts relative to three tremendous queries, namely:

1. Does the inward-man resemble the outward man?
2. Is the soul-man endowed with members, (hands, feet, bosom, tongue and eyes, etc?)
3. What happens to the five senses of man at death? If the corpse retained the senses it would, of necessity, become a ridiculous unthinkable thing akin to a zombie-like, dead-living-corpse.

What, then, does become of the five senses at physical death? We, most assuredly, have a right to know. God reveals this mystery in His Book. Allow Revelation, not speculation, to furnish the sought for information. The clattering nonsense of infidels (In-for-hells), though they are scheming self-styled scholars, positively will not suffice. Those who have the Satan-given right to explain away the Holy and Sacred Scriptures are neither competent thinkers nor capable Spirit-led Bible students.

Therefore the hellish-ranting's of demon possessed explain-away-the-Bible scholars (their own self appropriated title), to the truly born again believer, are strictly taboo.

The Bible Explains the Bible

The humble Bible reader secures his information by allowing the Bible to explain the Bible. He permits his mind to be enlightened as the Scriptures interpret the Scriptures.

The Spirit of Christ, architect of the miraculous miracle-book, the designer and builder of the universe, and universal man, knows how to talk intelligibly. The One who put the Book together certainly is sufficiently capable of telling us how He put man together.

Post Mortem

We have just received an urgent Dying-Man message which hurries us to the Modern City Hospital. Stepping off the elevator, on the third floor, we move quickly down the corridor, to the designated roam number.

What we see in the door way causes our hearts to sink with despair. A white clad doctor and a physician in a business suit are leaving the room. Two solemn faced attendants, followed by a sober looking intern and three grim faced nurses are wheeling an oxygen tank, a ventilator, and a respiratory apparatus from within the room.

The very demeanor of the doctors and the assistants, as well as the parade of equipment suggests the awful conclusion that these have fought and lost a desperate battle. The cold-breathed slinking last enemy, unseen and unnoticed slipped into that room. He, the "King of Terrors" won that appalling victory.

A shocking sight meets our gaze - this fear-some struggle had been won by that fearful monster who prepares man for the sepulcher. The awful result of that violent struggle is that that soul has been "Driven from light into darkness" (Job 18:18), and the body itself has been reduced to an ugly ashen corpse.

Where are the Five Senses?

Summoning a passing nurse, we request the presence of the attending Physician. We are about to make a startling inquiry: "Doctor," we begin, "I notice the terrible stare of the deceased; tell me, Sir, can this man see?" The Medic is taken aback at this, as is shown by his rejoinder.

One would hardly expect an expired patient to have the capacity of sight! But, I notice the fingers of the body are clutching at the bed clothing; my dear Doctor, can this one feel? I do not wait for an answer to this last, but quickly propose two more questions, as we stand beside the corpse:

The dead one still has the organs of hearing, "Sir, does he not hear? If not, what happens to the five senses at death?" Our friend of the Medical Profession blusters the announcement, "I have an urgent case down the hall. Please excuse me, Gentlemen!" We have great respect for Medical Science, and high esteem for the gallant men of that profession; but all stand aghast at our most proper, yet baffling, question: What happens to the Five Senses at Death?

Let us hold here for a moment. Soon the undertaker will arrive and prepare to remove the remains. I shall propound the same question to him and his assistant while they are placing the crumpled frame in the mortician's basket.

The Handler of the Dead Cannot Answer

If we expected a proper answer we are again disappointed, for the handler of the dead explains, "I'm afraid this sort of discussion is completely out of my line; but you might inquire of the lab-technician. He dissects the human body, you know."

Angels Cannot Answer

Our trip to the laboratory netted us very little, information, so, now, in desperation, we summon a holy angel to step down "Jacob's ladder" to conduct us on a tour through the Garden of Eden. We follow a winding path to the far side of this paradisiacal park, where our angelic conductor brings us to a sudden halt.

Work-Shop of the Universe

There, just ahead, beyond and outside the realm of the ordinary or normal, from our vantage point of revelation, our startled faith-eyes observe one of the grand spectacles of the creative events - the formation of the first human frame.

Creative power flowing through swiftly moving hands - the Creator Himself in the Work-Shop of the Universe - the race is being brought into being. Eyes, unaccustomed to viewing pre-time events, behold the Builder of man fashioning an external structure as a frame for the soul. The great transition: The miraculous, instantaneous passage of dust into flesh.

Form Still Lifeless

As we inspect the still, lifeless, physical structure, we stifle a desire to cry, "Why! This one cannot hear, neither can he see nor yet feel. He is most like the lifeless corpse we saw on the deathbed in the hospital". Our angel-conductor solemnly motions for deep silence as the Creator gently moves over the prostrate form to swiftly conclude this grand creative act.

Breath-Life Comes From God

He must animate the body-house by introducing and infusing that vigorous quality called life. To our utter amazement, this is accomplished by the builder pouring into the newly created vessel, His own divine "Breath of life."

Startled eyes observe the result: It is man's first life- breath. It is Adam's first heart-beat. Man's "breath-life" comes direct from God; man's heart-beat comes direct from God.

"Man O, man! Your breath-life comes from God. Your first heart-beat comes from God - and your second - and your third - and your thousandth - and every heart-beat". Your Creator-God must sustain you at every moment - and moment by moment, whether you wake or sleep; lest you die!

There! Adam is stirring! He lives, he is upon one knee. Alerted-man is now erect and standing before his Creator. He feels His glowing love - the warmth of his Maker's touch. He sees the hands of his Framer and Builder. He listens as the creative-voice calls him, "Adam!" "Adam," the grand title - what an honor is his! He is the first - the head of the human race.

The Five Senses Appear

There! There! There are the five senses in Adam! His lifeless form became awake after the infusion of God's vigorous life giving breath: Then, but, not until then, did the five senses appear. "And the Lord God formed (an intricate, but lifeless form) man of the dust of the ground, and breathed into his nostrils the breath of life (His life) and man became a living (more than mere animation, but conscious vigorous, five sense life) soul."

God's Created Image of Himself

The correct Latin word for the theological term "soul" (or nephesh) is anima; and this is from the Greek "anemos" - air or breath, because it is this which keeps the whole in life and in being.

What a notable and spectacular exhibition, this startling glimpse of the formation of the first human being. The physical fabrication provides a fearful and wonderful system-assemblage, where-by the soul can communicate with the physical world. Eye windows, that I might see out of my house. A built-in two-way public address system, that I might converse with the others of my kind.

Mystery Still Unsolved

True! There in Adam, and the sons of Adam, the Creator implanted five senses life: But! as yet, our great question is still unsolved. What happens to the five senses at death? Science cannot answer! Angels cannot answer!

Science, philosophy, man's wisdom, modern religion, and devil cults are all alike in this respect - unreliable answers. They are lost in a jungle of guesses. Satan as a marauding lion roars through this jungle seeking whom he may devour.

The Creator-Teacher Periscopes the Under-World
One should be most unwilling to trust this eternal question with any but the Eternal One. The Eternal Life steps down out of eternity to answer this ageless query, "What becomes of the five senses when death occurs?" He reveals the answer in a most unusual and startling manner. He allows a dead man to break the news to surprised and shocked earth-dwellers.

A Dead Man Answers
Remember, believer, the Creator of Adam indwells you! He is the Author of the Bible. So He dwells within you as your instructor. This is His method of revealing information. As you now read His own words, listen - listen! As the indwelling voice speaks to your own in-ward man!

"There was a certain rich man (any man) which was clothed in purple and fine linen, and fared sumptuously every day: And there was a certain beggar named Lazarus, which was laid at his gate full of sores, And desiring to be fed with the crumbs which fell from the rich man's table: Moreover the dogs carne and licked his sores!" (See Luke 16 for the Biblical account of this story.)

"And it came to pass that the beggar died and was carried by the angels into Abraham's bosom: the rich man also died, and was buried;" (Notice: the Instructor carefully informs us that one part of man is buried).

"And in Hell (unseen- Sheol-Hades world) he lift up his eyes (notice: the Lord said, 'eyes') being in torments (our problem is now, right here, solved - here are the five senses), and seeth (sense of sight) Abraham (been dead since B.C. 1857) afar off and Lazarus in his bosom (leaning upon Uncle Abraham's breast as he is welcomed and embraced)."

"And he cried (notice: the poor man talks) and said, Father Abraham, have mercy on me and send Lazarus that he may dip the tip of his finger (since one finger, he must have had all ten - also hands - arms - legs - in short a soul-body) in water (Lazarus feasting at the Lord's table, resting his head upon Abraham's bosom, drinking cool, clear, refreshing water from the Fountain of the Water of Life) for I (there's the "I" we have been looking for) am tormented (sense of feeling) in this flame (Jesus carefully chose this word, " flame"). But Abraham said, "Son, remember" (memory).

Dead Men Tell Tales
A Few Vivid Details of the Regions Below
Two men Dead: One a few seconds - the other a few hundred years. Both are alive and alert. Each know about, and are interested in, the upper world's activities. Abraham somehow seems to know that the "five brothers" have the Old Testament at their disposal, but do not believe it. Had they read Isaiah fourteen they would have known of their brother's dreadful plight at that very instant.

Abraham's name is well known to Heaven's citizens as well as on earth. The Lord gives us his name. But! The rich man? Unknown! Once a living-earth-being, now a being unknown - a disembodied soul - a savage ghost! He is now an ardent believer in the basic facts concerning life and death; Heaven and Hell, faith and unbelief; God and man. He learned in one awful moment that which he refused to learn in his life time.

He found no unbelievers in Hell. All unbelief is reserved for the world. He discovered no disbelievers will ever enter Hell or Heaven. All leave the world as converts. But! Alas! For many it will be too late.

Awful Thought!!!

That tormented man, at the moment you read this, is yet alive, down there still crying and wailing - "I am tormented - I thirst - I see - I hear - I now believe, but too late. I was pardoned from this awful place of agony, But, how awful! I rejected my pardon."

But permit the tormented five-sense-man, in Hell, tell his own story:

A Few Hell-Chosen Words

This, now converted, man in Hell is very active in that he prepares a message (a funeral message) and wants it delivered to his five brothers by special delivery. Here, then, is one letter posted in Hell. You say, This message was never delivered. Oh, but, it was. Who, it may be interesting to inquire, was the postman?

As incredible as it may appear, Jesus, in grace, Dear Reader, delivered that message. There it is on the pages of Holy Writ (See Luke 16:19-31), for all brothers left behind. May it serve as an eternal warning!

A Scorching Funeral Message From the Pit:

> Unknown Soul,
> Hades,
> Torment Section.
> A.D. 33
> Five Brothers, Jerusalem, Palestine.
>
> Dear Five Brothers:
>   As you tearfully stand about my fearfully emancipated body - while it still lies upon my death couch, swollen tongue protruding, bony fingers clutching at

the bed clothing, glassy eyes staring at nothing, you may wonder, "What has happened to our brother?"

"Where is he? What is he doing? Does he remember? Does he care? What has happened to the five senses? Is he trying to get a message thru to us?" Listen brothers, each of you! I am screaming, bellowing, and crying this message to Abraham. He has been dead centuries, But I see him there across the gulf. He is talking with me now.

Do you remember the beggar at our gate? When he died they hauled his body off to the dump heap (in fact I'm the one who ordered his body to be cast there), he is with Abraham in comfort, now he is a multi-millionaire.

Let me list my torments in terms of my five senses:

1. I am tormented in this flame - (sense of feeling).
2. I see Abraham afar off (sense of sight for I have eyes).
3. I just heard Abraham say, 'Son, remember' (hearing and memory).
4. I beg for water (sense of taste).
5. I am tormented in fire and brimstone (I can smell the sulfuric fumes).

Thus you see, Lost Brothers, the five senses are embedded, not in the flesh-body, but in the eternal soul-ish (ghost) body. As frightful as this may seem, this ghost-body keeps crying eternally. This ghost-body (soul or inward man) has substance and form, yet is invisible to the physical eye. The members of this soul-body are eyes, ears, and vocal cords, fingers, tongue, bosom, etc. I know this may frighten you, But! I have survived the physical body; I talk, remember, cry, wail, weep, hate, and suffer untold torments.

Listen, boys, physical life is the soul's career in the body. Death is the soul's career out of the body. The in-ward-man is just as much alive after death as he was before he died. All these, here in the Pit, were frightfully surprised to learn that the desires of the physical body, live on in the soul after he expires.

Terror in the Execution Chamber: Blazing Points to Ponder
Pardons are not obtainable after death. Unbelief reigns only on the earth. Two things are absolutely worthless on the earth, a ghost and a corpse. A ghost is a soul without the body. A corpse is a body without the soul.

The Bible's description of Hell is true. I did not stand before God when I died. God knew I was condemned already. God knew I was not His child by the new birth. I never accepted Him as my Savior. He knew I did not accept Him. The five senses stay with the man.

On earth there is an admixture of good and bad. Down here there is no mixture - it is all bad. There is a place where all is good. Oh! Why did I miss that place? Near me a bellowing ghost is attempting suicide. No use! Some, though, who have been here for centuries, still try it.

Death changed only my address. Lust-habits, and evil desires stay with the man. These only add to our torments. We down here do not have eternal life. Pit-dwellers have everlasting existence.

One lost soul thought he had been down here three thousand years. He let out a hellish shriek when he learned that a day is as a thousand years down here. Pit dwellers are living-dead people.

Whoever reads this, although they do so centuries after my incarceration, let them understand I will, at that very moment, still be here, shrieking, in the underworld. I thought it stylish and refined, and a mark of intelligence not to believe in this infernal place. But! Down here we are known as fools. Eternal fools! In conclusion I must say, "This is but for one night. One terrifying eternal night!

Your Tormented Brother.

P.S. Think of it! Six brothers in my father's house; one in Hell, five on the way!

One Person in Three

Remember please, this area of our book is dealing with the mystery of one person in three. This is a reference to the three in one unit called man - God's created image of Himself. Thus far our examination of this mysterious creature has been confined mainly to the physical-body and soul body. But, now we pursue the Scriptural investigation of the spirit-body.

Lest some look askance at this reference to the soul as a body, I need only remind them that in Luke 16, Jesus showed us a dead man's body in the grave. Immediately, our infallible Teacher pulls aside the curtain and allows us to look beyond the buried body to see the unknown lost man in torment. There, in the City of Ghosts, we find these non-physical bodied men with eyes, tongue, vocal cords and ears, as well as other instruments. They display emotion, concern, tear, memory, five senses, and fearful sufferings. Does not all this certainly suggest a soul-body?

The above description of Mr. "Rich Mans" lost soul is not a man's own interpretation; But! Jesus' own interpretation. Would any man dare interpret Jesus' own interpretation? The Bible is God's own explanation and interpretation of eternal spiritual truths.

Spirit – Soul - Body

"And I pray God your whole spirit and soul and body be preserved blameless unto the coming of our Lord Jesus Christ." (1 Thessalonians 5:23). Thus we find man is a tripartite, having three corresponding parts or copies. By virtue of the soul, man is self-conscious. By the power of the physical-body he is world conscious. Through the medium of the spirit, one has God consciousness.

Without the earth-body, man, can no longer possess world consciousness; although still self-conscious, undressed from world-body organs (ears, eyes, etc.), one cannot see, hear or smell, taste or feel that which the world has to offer.

Therefore, for the same reason, neither can Heaven reveal sights, wonders, sounds and ecstasies to the person who is dead spiritually. As a blind and deaf man cannot see or hear physical sights and sounds, so spirit-dead man can neither see and hear nor feel the offerings of Heaven.

What the earth-body is to the soul, while on earth, so the spirit-body is to the soul in Heaven. The unregenerate man, and the born again man are both subject to physical death. Neither can dwell in the same earth-body with the King of Terrors (death). When the great move comes, both must change address.

The Christian has a spirit-body from Heaven, therefore he moves from earth to dwell in the heavenly realm. The poor unsaved, not having a born-from-Heaven body, can neither see nor enter the Kingdom (John 3:3,5).

Disembodied Ghosts
There is but one awful place in the Universe for a soul who neither has a physical-body nor a spirit-body; the asylum of the universe. There the disembodied ghost becomes a weeping, wailing, raving, maniac.

The blessed Savior offers to His blood bought ones the miracle of the mysterious new birth. Those who refuse or postpone the new birth from above, until it is too late, will discover to their own awful amazement that they have desecrated and profaned their own soul. Don't be tied to the post of postponement.

First Birth: Earth-Body. Second Birth: Heaven-body.
Well that makes good sense! First time I was born I received an earthy-body that I might live on the earth. The second birth gave me a body from Heaven in order that I might dwell there. How long could I live on this earth if torn from my earthly body? Not one moment! How long could a person live in Heaven without a heavenly body? Not one moment! Thus, the Master taught, "Ye must be born again" (John 3:3).

"For we know (positively) that if our earthly house of this taber-nacle (transient shelter - temporary) were dissolved (decomposed to melt back into the earth), we (the born from above ones) have a building (for the soul) of God, an house not made with hands (Adam's earth-house-body made by hands - Creator's hands), eternal (contrast this with earthly tabernacle) in the Heavens (eternal heavenly materials) (2 Corinthians 5:1).

"For in this we groan, earnestly desiring to be clothed upon with our house which is from Heaven (notice: clothed upon - house from heaven.) If so be that being clothed we shall not be found naked (soul nakedness - having neither earth-body nor heaven- body)" (2 Corinthians 5:2-3).

"For we that are in this tabernacle do groan (old age, tooth ache, heart aches) being burdened: not for that we would be unclothed (most awful agony in the universe is to be disembodied) but Clothed upon (notice: clothed upon), that mortality might be swallowed up of life" (2 Corinthians 5:4)

Jesus said, "That which is born of the Spirit is spirit" (John 3:6). By virtue of the first birth I receive a house from the earth. When born again I receive a house from Heaven.

Paul caught up to the Spirit Realm: A Tour of heaven

Paul was permitted to reveal to us but one soul thrilling detail of his tour of the Third Heaven (Paradise). Although it would have been unlawful for him to describe the glories he saw or the unspeakable words he heard, he is permitted, of the Spirit, to reveal one mystery. "I Knew a man in Christ above fourteen years ago, (whether in the body, I cannot tell, or whether out of the body, I cannot tell: God knoweth); such a one caught up to the Third Heaven (See 2 Corinthians 12:2-6).

"And I knew such a man, (whether in the body, or out of the body, I cannot tell: God knoweth);" "How he was caught up into Paradise, and heard unspeakable words, which it is not lawful for a man to utter."

Paul, what is this one thing you are permitted to reveal? When you stepped up Jacob's Ladder and walked through John's door of Revelation 4:1, and toured Heaven, what did you see that so startled you, that God had to send a messenger of Satan to buffet you, lest you be exalted above measure?

I can imagine Paul's answer: "Folks, I can tell you this much, those folk up there look just like we do down here. I looked them over, and looked myself over, while up there, and for the life of me, to this day, I cannot tell whether I was in the body or out."

Evidently, then, the House from Heaven looks just like our earth-bodies; only, of course, the Heaven-body is perfect, yet an exact pattern of the other. What a comfort to know and understand our dear loved ones, over yonder, are the same and appear the same as they did down here. Only, of a surety we may know, their spirit-houses are not marred by sin, time, or disease. Glory!

The Mystery of Life Before Birth: When Does Life's Journey Begin?
We know eternal life enters into man at Calvary. But! When does natural life begin? At the moment of physical birth? Just prior to that birth? If prior, how much prior? Do the Scriptures answer this most perplexing, and yet all important, pre-natal question? Yes, very definitely, God's eternal law has the answer, full and complete. It is there in Holy Writ for all to consider in the light of His great love.

All peoples, everywhere, should know the full and startling answer as to when they become a person or soul in the sight of God. Allow the following Spirit endowed words to convey to your startled perception a truth, seemingly, unknown to many. Hidden away in the store-house of His profound secrets is this amazing revelation. May your soul be enlightened with the brilliancy of His illuminating Word-Light. Honestly! His great love amazes us as we behold His care and attention of a little unborn one.

Where Did I Come From? How Long Have I Been Here?
"Thine eyes did see my substance, yet being imperfect (incomplete); and in Thy Book all my members were written which in continuance were fashioned, when as yet there was none of them." "Thou hast possessed my

reins: Thou hast covered me in my mother's womb." "My substance was not hid from Thee when I was made in secret." (Psalm 139:13-16).

God saw you in your mother's womb; when you were still, mind you, substance. Before you were formed, He saw you. "Yet being imperfect" (incomplete). He not only saw you, but, covered you. You see! You were conceived in sin and shaped in iniquity (Psalm 51:5).

Therefore the great and loving God covered you - possessed you - and wrote up a description of you. When? While still substance, Where? In your mother's womb! How soon after conception? While still a secret to all but God. Your God saw you even while still a secret to your parents, even your physician. He saw you and a description written of you in His Book when as yet you were still unformed.

A Startling Consideration

The premature death of that little body, being formed, would send the tiny soul to be with the Father in Heaven. He covered it with His love and grace. This, then, was His method for handling original sin. A heavenly record has been made of a soul and its earthly frame being formed in the womb of the mother.

God Even Possessed It

Should that written record reveal the purposeful premature destruction of that little one, it would be there as a thundering accusation against those who plotted that that tiny one should never be permitted to see the light of this world.

The Loving Heavenly Father saw it, wrote up a description of its future aspect (this is even greater than recording its name) and in grace covered it. Why? Why did God do this? Because it was a tiny soul! An eternal Soul! Amen!

Had the great and tender Father not seen it, since it was a secret to all others, there would have been no one to love it, until later. Is it possible that our Father, who takes notice of even the falling sparrow would leave unnoticed and unloved, anywhere in His big universe, a tiny unknown soul? Unthinkable! God forbid!

Study, Discussion & Application Points for Chapter 2

1. Read and study this chapter.

2. Key verse for this chapter is 1 Thessalonians 5:23: *"And the very God of peace sanctify you wholly; and I pray God your whole spirit and soul and body be preserved blameless unto the coming of our Lord Jesus Christ."*

3. Many will operate under the premise that they are a body with a soul. Dr. Lambert declares it is the opposite that is true; we are souls with a body. How might this thought affect our priorities? Look at these passages that underscore this truth and jot down your reflections:
   - Genesis 2:7
   - 2 Corinthians 5:1, 6-8

4. Dr. Lambert uses the story of the Rich Man and Lazarus (found in Luke 16:19-31) as proof of our conciseness after death. Look at this passage and write down each mention of the five senses. How does this affect your perception of heaven and hell?

5. Our First Birth involved physical life and our Second Birth involved our spiritual life or heaven body. Look at the following passages and write down the main thought(s) for each verse (note: quickened = made alive):
   - John 3:6-7
   - Ephesians 2:1, 5

6. Scripture tells us each person is made in the image of God. Much of our longing for and capacity for spiritual things is deeply entwined in our nature. The quest for God rests deep within a seeker's soul. Consider these passages concerning our creation and jot down your findings:
   - Psalm 139:13-16
   - Genesis 1:26-27
   - Romans 1:19-20

3

THE MYSTERY OF
THE INDWELLING CHRIST

The Theatre of the Universe: A Baffling Mystery in Two Acts

Two Actors: Christ and You
Time: In the beginning.

Act One: Christ in His Universe

With the brilliancy of eternity's searchlight focused upon the spacious empty stage of limitless expanse; we behold the central figure of creation's drama, resplendent in His robes of glory, just a step from His celestial throne: With uplifted hand, and by the power of His word, He orders a universe into being.

Out of empty nothingness, worlds spring into existence; planets begin spinning in their orbits; suns begin their battles with darkness along their circuits; stars begin running their time-baffling courses. That which was once unlimited emptiness is now crowded with millions of galaxies, with only firmaments to separate them. The curtain runs down on one of the mighty creative acts of the ageless past.

Act Two: Christ in you

Again the stage is set: We have come down the stairway of time. As holy angels watch intently from Heaven's balcony, another figure is brought into focus. He kneels and calls upon God for salvation. Who is this petitioner? One moment, Dear Christian Reader, and you shall see!

Ah! There! Now we see more clearly. (A delightful surprise awaits you). The stage, this time, is a simple altar in a church. Again the mighty and majestic Creator steps from His Heavenly Throne. Proceeding to the yonder kneeling one, He waits quietly as the solicitor prays. The Creator is about to create a "New Creature."

Mystery of mysteries! Wonder of wonders! Our hearts are shocked! Our souls immeasurably thrilled at the unparalleled spectacle displayed before our eyes. The Creator Himself just joined and coalesced Himself with the body of this new believer. Christ now dwells within. Hear the angels applaud; listen as the appraising choirs of Heaven rejoice - hallelujah! Amen! And ten-thousand more hallelujahs!

We are about to learn the identity of that soul - the one in whom the mighty God just dwelt Himself. His name has just been entered into the ponderous book of God Almighty- listen as even the angels listen - they have just learned the "Mystery of the ages is, Christ in you." You, dear reader are the one that is the "New Creature" upon your asking Christ within.

Stupendous thought: One day the Creator brought this Universe into existence; one day, millenniums later, this One moved into you. "Christ in you, the hope of glory." The Author and Maker of Creation are actually, personally and literally "in" you. Here is something that excites wonder, stimulating, awe-inspiring, fearfully superior, a resplendent and magnificent revelation. Believer! Christ is in you.

You may in astonishment cry, "Am I to believe that the Almighty, the Maker of Heaven and Earth, the God of Abraham, Isaac and Jacob, dwells Himself in actuality within my own body"? Yes, Dear Christian, if you are a blood bought, redeemed one, the answer is a soul stimulating yes. He dwells eternally in you.

"Christ in you" is no mere interpretation of men. Although words cannot properly convey the true magnitude of this profound mystery, it is no exaggeration (yet so it may seem), these are the exact words of Scripture: "Christ in you, the hope of glory" (Colossians 1:27). Amen!

If this be true, Christian, then Christ is just as much in you as you are in you. He is in your body to exactly the same measure as you are in your body. He is just as real in you as you are real in you. Just as surely as you dwell in your body, just as certainly, He dwells in there with you. Beloved, if this be true, and no exaggeration, then the great mystery is revealed. It is revealed to you when you believe. When you believe it to be so, because God's Word says so; just then the mystery is ended and it becomes a revelation!

Are You Shock Proof?
Brother, if that does not bless and stir you and excite you to the very depths of your soul, then you are just simply shock proof. We should react as though a dynamite blast had suddenly been set off in the midst of our inner being. Let us praise Him for revealing this match-less and soul thrilling truth! Glory! Amen!

A Double Mystery: Christ in You, You in Christ
"At that day ye shall know that I am in My Father, and ye in Me, and I in you." (John 14:20). Allow the full import of this startling statement grip your heart. Here is a mystery within a mystery. Christ in you, you in Christ. Our minds inquire; could this possibly be so? Can I be in Him and He in me?

The Tiny Preposition "In"
Let us examine these extremely mystifying words which fell from the Master Teacher's lips. Notice the preposition in; it is a tiny word; but, carries an eternal load of meaning. "At that day ye shall know that I am in my Father and ye in Me, and I - in you."

Our Lord's statement is most startling, it asserts something, which at first, seems to defy one's efforts to comprehend; could it at all possibly be so? Does our Lord mean exactly what He says? Child of God, does not our Lord always mean just what He says? Are we not always to believe Him, and to take at face value every word of every statement? Are not Jesus' teachings an interpretation of eternity's mysteries?

Let us, then, listen again, let us believe each word; let us neither be baffled nor unbelieving. Human reasoning can never attain unto the heights of God's thoughts. As we ponder the meaning of these mysteries, we must never turn aside from God's own revelations to the speculative claptrap of mere men. Our Savior not only urges us to believe Him for the very works sake, but, He hastens to inform us, "At that day ye shall know" (understand the mystery of the indwelling Christ).

Let us not read sentences only, rather, may we read a word at a time. Each word is a thought to be carefully considered. We should eat of the bread of life a bite at a time. Jesus says, "If a man loves Me, he will keep My words: and My Father and I will come unto him, and make our abode with him" (John 14:23).

The Upper Room: A Wonderful Object Lesson – A Demonstration
Doubtless the Apostles, themselves, marveled at the Master's assertion - it was so astonishing. Their hearts, like ours, might well inquire, how can these things be? May the Holy Spirit make real to us, through this demonstration, that which the Word teaches is so!

The Lord had been crucified and buried. The frightened, bewildered disciples had locked themselves within the Upper Room. "Then the same day at evening, being the first day of the week, when the doors were shut where the disciples were assembled for tear of the Jews, came Jesus and stood in their midst, and saith unto them, Peace be unto you" (John 20:19).

Christ in the Wall – The Wall in Him
Pretend, dear reader, you were also in the upper room, in company with the Apostles that day; suddenly Jesus appears in the midst. You are

startled at first, and then you wonder, how did He gain entrance? The verse, above, is very careful to inform that the doors were shut. He did not pass through an open door, but, doubtless, through the wall itself.

A Miracle Performed

Now, for a crude, but the writer hopes, a helpful and illuminating illustration: Consider that for a moment the risen Lord stood in the midst of the wall (you will agree that Jesus for one little moment was in the wall and the wall in Him as He stepped into the room). You see the sense in Which He would have been in the wall and the wall in Him? Does this not, Christian, assist in perceiving that in like manner He has fused Himself with your being? Thus He is in you, and you in Him.

You perceive, then, the Lord Jesus, our most adorable Redeemer, did mean exactly what He said. At the moment you received Him as Savior He stepped over into you, clothed Himself upon you, and fused His own Person with yours. Now, it is literally, actually, gloriously true, the two of you have become one. "I in them, and Thou in Me, that they may be made perfect in one". (John 17:23).

Now observe the following, and manifold other verses spring into more wonderful meaning: "If any man be in Christ he is a new creature." God has made of "Twain one new man" (See 2 Corinthians 5:17 and Ephesians 2:15) Unfolded mystery, Christ in you, the hope of glory!

A Startling Question

Is He just a little Christ, dwelling in your heart only, or is He of full stature covering you with His presence; your whole being? We must surely see that if we are in Him, He must surely be of full stature to cover us with His dwelling presence. That being true, the mystery of the ages becomes an even more surprising and magnificent revelation than we dared to suppose at first.

The dwelling within of Christ is not just a power or influence

We must not de-personalize the Christ by making Him to be just a power or influence; our minds must not compress Him, as it were, by making Him a little Christ just large enough to dwell in a tiny space no larger than our heart.

In a recent Bible class, one of His dear ones remarked, "Oh! I'm so glad to know that Christ indwells us to our exact size." She had found the secret of the indwelling Christ. Does not this most momentous and heart moving mystery fill your very soul with glory and amazement? Allow, then, the following verse to further excite your wonder! "For it is God which worketh in you both to will and to do of His good pleasure". (Philippians 2:13).

God works in you creating a willingness to please Him. Actually, though, it is His willingness you feel in your heart. His blessed heart beats within yours. He loves through your heart and thinks through your mind (you do have the Mind of Christ - 1 Corinthians 2:16).

He does not say, "imitate Me"; rather, He invites Himself to come into and control your very being and think through your mind His own thoughts; and work in you, and by His power you also, will please the Father by putting those thoughts into deeds.

The Mystery of Salvation is Not Having Mine Own Righteousness but Christ's

Apart from the indwelling Christ there is no salvation. Heaven's law, given by way of Mount Sinai, demands perfection. "Thou art of purer eyes than to behold evil, and canst not look on iniquity" (Habakkuk 1:13).

God cannot look upon sin with any degree of allowance; God's glory is His perfection He cannot compromise with the sinner by lowering His standard. How, then, can imperfect man ever find the way to Heaven? Divine love and omniscient wisdom coupled with omnipotence finds a way; it is, "Christ in you, the hope of glory."

While the law (Ten Commandments) is God's written standard of perfection, the Son is His living standard. Christ, living within you, has thus met God's (and Heaven's) demand for your perfection, perfectly. He condescended to live within us to give that perfection.

Glory! Christ is now living His perfect life within you, day by day, while crediting it to your account daily. Amen!

The Apostle Paul did not trust his own righteousness; although in Philippians 3:4-6, he declared; "If any other man thinketh that he hath whereof he might trust in the flesh, I more," But with strong delight exhorted others to rejoice in their new standing in the Lord; His perfection credited to their account in Heaven.

With rapture Paul cries, "And be found in Him, not having mine own righteousness, which is of the law, but that which is through the faith of Christ, the righteousness Which is of God by faith" (Philippians 3:9).

We are Made Acceptable in Him
With joy unspeakable the Apostle expounded this profound mystery by declaring, "He hath made us acceptable in Him." Notice, Lover of Christ, Made acceptable in Him. How often this wee preposition appears on the pages of Holy Writ: In Him, Christ in you, you in the Beloved.

Sinners though we are, yet in loving condescension our Loving Savior dwells His perfection within. This is in order that He may credit to our account, His holiness. What an extravagant love-gift. This soul exhilarating and priceless truth should so stimulate our whole being as to cause us to cry with Paul, "I can do all things through Christ which strengtheneth me" (Philippians 4:13). I can now resist sin through Him. I can stand fast in the power of His might.

He Becomes You with You
During a lecture on the above subject, at the Tulsa Baptist Temple, I asked the able and talented Pastor, the Rev. Clifford Clark to stand before the audience while I addressed him in this manner:

"Mr. Clark, your Savior, the Lord Jesus, has moved into you to become Clifford Clark with you. He is not just a little Christ who dwells in your heart only, but, of full stature. He; covers you to become you with you. "Do you not know that your 'body is the temple of the Holy

Ghost' who abides in you and has thus made you acceptable in God's sight by giving to you His righteousness."

"He not only was your stand-in or substitute when He died for you on the cross, but, He also assumed the guilt of your sins, centuries before you even sinned them. However, back there on Calvary He is, one day, to become you, with you, by being in you; so, back there, potentially you were in Him; and now, you can shout in the devil's face, and cry with Paul, "I am crucified with Christ" (Galatians 2:20).

"Your punished Creator, who experienced the cross, can now, also: create within you the reality of the fact of this cross-death experience. By appropriating the power of the might of this cross-experience, the redeemed Christian can resist the puny strength of every foe."

Interpolation
The Rev. Mr. Clark, Pastor of one of America's largest and most spiritual churches, is a dear friend to the author. Eternity, alone, will permit full time to repay this Dear Brother. I predict God will use Clifford Clark to build one of the largest churches in the country!

Study, Discussion & Application Points for Chapter 3

1. Read and study this chapter.
2. The key verse for this chapter is Colossians 1:27: "To whom God would make known what is the riches of the glory of this mystery among the Gentiles; which is Christ in you, the hope of glory".
3. Perhaps it is difficult to understand Christ's words in John 14:20: "and ye in Me, and I in you". However, if you heard that a ship sunk to the bottom of the ocean, which is true: "The boat is in the water" or "Water is in the boat". The obvious answer is both are true. With that said, Dr. Lambert brings forth this truth by having us reflect on the following verses. Please read and write your thoughts down.

- 2 Corinthians 5:17
- 2 Corinthians 13:5
- John 17:23
- 1 Corinthians 2:16

4. Dr. Lambert points out that one of the marvelous blessings of the Indwelling Christ is that we now share His righteous nature.   Consider these passages and then jot down your thoughts:
   - Philippians 3:9
   - 2 Corinthians 5:21

5. The presence of Christ in our life is more than just a power or influence. As the little guy said "If I'm four feet tall and Jesus is six feet tall and He lives inside me; then Jesus should be sticking out all over!" Look at the following verses that indicate the spiritual work that Christ is doing through us:
   - Philippians 2:13
   - Philippians 4:13
   - Romans 8:10-11
   - Ephesians 2:10
   - Colossians 1:27-29

6. A Holy God demands perfection and yet, we are flawed. Consider new found confidence as we consider how the presence of Christ has changed our nature from sinful to righteous:
   - Hebrews 4:16
   - Ephesians 3:12
   - 1 John 2:28
   - 1 John 3:21

4

THE MYSTERY OF THE BORN AGAIN SPIRIT: THE CHRISTIAN IS A SPIRIT-MAN

Y ou, Christian, are a spirit-man. "That which is born of the Spirit is spirit." (John 3:6). A spirit-man is an eternal being - as the angels. You are a new creature; you, as a spirit-creature are something very special.

Look away, startled one, from the pages of this book, for a moment. Take a look into the land of endless days. Take into thoughtful account the full import of our Savior-Creator's time-shattering annunciation, "That which is born of the Spirit is Spirit."

Since you are born of the Spirit, you are a spirit! But! This is not the full end of this stupendous thought. You, a citizen of two worlds, are a combination-of the celestial and terrestrial - something from earth - something from Heaven. Not of the earth for the earth alone, but of the heavens for the heavens as well – a new creature of eternity, dwelling in time.

Created Twice
The Creator created you twice. The first time He made you an earth-being - the last time a spirit-being, like an angel. You have now been translated into the kingdom of His dear Son. This may be verified by reading Colossians 1:13.

That kingdom is a realm of spirits, Angels, Cherubim, and born again spirits. You are a part of that realm; having become a spirit yourself. Powerful spirits are all about you, some holy and some evil (for evil spirits are in the realm of spirit) are now your companions and your adversaries.

The Master is delivering the devil a terrific head bruising blow as He instructs the new born Christian, you are a born of the Spirit creature. Unfathomable wisdom, stupendous power, has combined that which is eternal with that which is temporal, and the full result is: that new creature is a spirit-man.

Eternity Dwells in You

This next mystery must be softly spoken, lest its atomic-thrust colliding with your sensibilities leave you reeling with absolute amazement. Allow Him to whisper into your soul this secret which belongs to eternity.

This eternal spirit part of you is without beginning. It has always been – will always be. This part is now essentially a very part of you. Your eternal self had no beginning, and is without ending. You now dwell in eternity. Eternity dwells in you!

You have entered into something that had neither beginning nor ending- rather that something has entered into you. As the physical creation, from the earth, is temporal; so the Spirit creation is from out of eternal materials that had no beginning and can have no ending. Therefore, your eternal-spirit is without a beginning! God gave you something at your new birth which is of eternal quality - which quality is life.

That part of you is spirit. You now possess something that never had a beginning. This eternal spirit attached itself to you, now is a part of you, thus you are now forever a new-creature of eternity - A spirit-man. Here, then, is something new - brand-new, a something that cannot grow old - new – and always will be new. Amen!

Creator-Savior

Only a Creator could be a Savior. Our dear Savior must of necessity be the Creator. Whoever undertakes to save a sinner must be a Creator in order to create him a new creation. This eternal spirit which He has put in you cannot die. Could an eternal thing die? Could eternity ever be less than forever? Can fire freeze?

"In the Lord is everlasting strength" (Isaiah 26:4). In order to live forever, one must possess a strength that can withstand the rigors of eternal duration. Only a spirit made of eternal qualities could thus possess everlasting strength. In fact, the source of life must indwell him. Please remember, unsaved have everlasting existence. But, only the Christian possesses Eternal Life. Eternal Life is Jesus Himself! He is the very source of life! All who are born into this world are passing through nature into eternity.

Mortality Swallowed Up of Life

Life is something from out of eternity that swallows up time. When eternal life begins temporal life ceases. This is death and the entering into of eternal life. By merging The Eternal Spirit with man's born again spirit, Omnipotence has forged a new creation, an eternal Spirit-Man.

Who would not trade temporal life for eternal life? Eternal life is taking that which never had a beginning, will never have an ending, putting it into a mortal being; thus "mortality is swallowed up of life."

Existed Before Calvary

Consider this amazing truth! If there is a part of me which had no beginning - even lived before Calvary - then it could have been nailed to the cross! Now! I can in great triumph cry with Paul, "I am crucified with Christ." This, then, is the mystery of the ages, Christ in you, the hope of glory!

A Divine and wonderful Resident, from the realm of eternity, now dwells with me in my body. "He who hath the Son hath life." (1 John 5:12). He, then, is my eternal life. He is that Eternal Life which was with the Father (1 John 1:2). He, The Eternal One, without beginning or ending, has now become a part of me. May Praise be His for ever and ever!

The Christ-in-one elevated to celestial glory, can shout in the face of trials, temptations, and tribulations, "For I reckon that the sufferings of this present time are not to be compared with the glory which shall be revealed "in us" (Romans 8:18).

The Mystery of Eternal Life, Not Mere Endless Life

We shall now see that eternal life is not mere quantity - rather, quality. Eternal-life, for the believer, is the Eternal Christ abiding (dwelling forever) in the being of that One. "He that hath the Son hath Life."

Eternal Life is not mere endlessness; for even the unsaved have everlasting existence: But! The Christian has a quality of life announced by the Life Giver as "Life more abundant."

Eternal Life is a Person

Let us not enter too hastily into this next soul-rocker, unless, by chance, you may be equipped with spiritual shock-absorbers. The sudden collision of the following truth with our mental powers of absorption is mighty apt to horribly mutilate the unregenerate, and deliver the hindering devil crushing injuries, if not leave him with a stroke of paralysis.

These vital, basic, enduring, devil-chasing words were uttered by Satan's Master to impart spiritual vigor and sin-killing vitality to the sluggish soul: Jesus declared, "I am the Life." Eternal Life then, is a Person. "We know that the Son of God is come, and we are in Him that is true, even His Son Jesus Christ. This is the true God, and eternal life. This, the true God, is Eternal Life" (1 John 5:20). Our God is here referred to as Eternal Life. God is eternal; God is life, hence Eternal Life. The individual in Him is in eternal life.

Life is More Than Activity or Consciousness

Life is more than animation, activity or even consciousness. Time-life is physical or organic life. The Christian or Christ-in-one has both, time-life and Eternal-Life. Whereas, the unregenerate man has time-life, yet from and at the moment of disembodiment or cessation of earthy-organic life, and on forever he still possesses existence-life. He must endure for the period of duration of the existence of God (infinite duration), self-imposed incarceration in the City of Ghosts.

This lost-one, unknown in Heaven, has now come to the end of time-life, and by virtue of death has begun endless-life! This ghost-being is still full of animation, consciousness, and the vital senses. He has not ceased to exist. He will never be reduced to nothing. He is in his soul-body, dwelling amid the detestable, repulsive, violently mad inmates of the Asylum of the Universe.

These incurables must remain imprisoned for the duration of God's existence. They are there for two main reasons:

> First - They sinned and still desire to sin. If released, no matter where their abode (earth or Heaven), they would seek opportunity to sin. They are not cured of the sin-disease; only the New Birth could do that.
> Second - They cannot live on earth because their firstborn-physical body is no longer tenantable. It has another tenant; the Dean of Horrors who with repulsive appetite razes that house, reducing it to a mass of corruption, before it returns to the dust. They cannot dwell in Heaven for the same reason they cannot dwell on earth - no spirit or heaven-body.

Jesus' teachings certify the power of endless and continuous life is a very part of the indissoluble structural make-up of the human soul. The person who is victimized by error or unbelief will not be physically dead ten seconds until the awful discovery that the Spirit's interpretation of death, in such passages as Luke 16:19-31, as well as Isaiah 14:9-11, coupled with Revelation 14:9-13, as well as host of others, is true and accurate after all. In spite of all Satan called ministers, whose brassy clattering and serpentine writings have wrested the Scriptures and plain teachings of the Word of God, the Bible's description of Hell and death conforms to the truth of these matters after all.

There are two excellent methods by which one may accurately ascertain the true facts concerning death and hell: One is to read them in the Scriptures, while the other is to verify them upon arrival at the Gates of the Damned! This is self-inflicted torment!

Life is More Than Continuance of Existence

Let us not lose sight of the main consideration in this area of our book: Eternal life is more than everlasting survival. Everlasting existence became yours by right of the first birth - that was your beginning. But, by virtue of the second birth you possess eternal life which has no beginning, as well as no ending. Jesus Christ, who is from everlasting to everlasting, the Alpha and Omega, dwells His eternal life in the being of the regenerated believer.

To eternize an earth-born-being would necessitate the introduction of an eternal being into that one. Might one suggest the infusion of an angelic spirit with this mortal? No! We must immediately reject this startling suggestion, upon the grounds, angels had a beginning.

A mental bomb-burst is found in the first four words of the Holy Bible, "In the beginning God." Christian! In order that God might give you eternal life, He must forge a new creation in Christ, the eternal One, merging Himself with your being; Christ in you, the hope of glory!

To inspirit God, in a time-born believer, is to eternize a mortal. "But if the Spirit of Him that raised up Jesus from the dead dwell in you, He that raised up Christ from the dead shall also quicken your mortal bodies by His Spirit that dwelleth in you" (Romans 8:11). Astonishing! A native of earth, a native of Heaven!

"For it is God which worketh in you both to will and do of His good pleasure." (Philippians 2:13). When this Divine Guest moves into an earth dweller, immediately that one is roused and stimulated by eternal motives. Time-things lose their control; the heart is energized by new and holy desires.

What is this that has so suddenly revolutionized the born again believer? Is it not the indwelling One introducing Himself? He is manifesting His own person in the presence chamber of your heart. You know He is abiding in your body, for He is reproducing, in you, His intense desire to reach the precious lost ones.

He is producing in you that which is in Himself; His eyes looking through surrendered eyes onto a field white unto harvest. His mind merged with the believer's mind to give him the "Mind of Christ."

He is making you willing to obey the Father's command, by allowing you to feel His own will and intense desire to obey every loving demand of your God. He permits His own willing and obedient heart to beat through the surrendered heart of His child. He wishes intently, through that heart, to follow the Spirit's leading.

He also donates His own strength of force enabling that one to follow through and carry out those inward desires; For it is God which worketh in you both to will and to do of His good pleasure and to make you willing to allow Him to do it. "Being confident of this very thing, that He which hath begun a good work in you will perform it until the day of Jesus Christ" (See Philippians 1:5 & 2:13). This is life! Abundant life!

The Eternal Christ allows His vigorous, powerful, resurrected life flow through those in whom He abides. Forcible and intense revolutionizing desires now energize the will. This is God's method of creating obedience in the surrendered soul! The one who relinquishes his own will, and thus resigns his person into the power of the abiding Christ, is Living! Living the life more abundant!

Study, Discussion & Application Points for Chapter 4

1. Read and study this chapter.
2. The key verse for this chapter is Colossians 1:13 *"Who hath delivered us from the power of darkness, and hath translated us into the kingdom of his dear Son:"*

3. Dr. Lambert asserts that "only a Creator could be a Savior. Whoever undertakes to save a sinner must be a Creator in order to create him a new creation." Consider the implications of Jesus being our Creator/Savior.
   - Read Colossians 1:13-19 and record your thoughts.
   - Read 2 Corinthians 5:17 and record your thoughts.

4. Upon our conversion, we have been "born again" or created a second time. This new creation includes our "spirit-man" which will live eternally. Read and study 1 Corinthians 15:38-46 and note the two bodies. As you read this passage, ask the Lord to be your teacher and record your thoughts.

5. Our natural body was created for this earth and has a certain "shelf-life". In time, we all see our bodies succumb to age, illness and disease. It's obvious that our natural (physical) body is not built to withstand the glory and greatness of heaven. Read and study 1 Corinthians 15:50-57 and record your thoughts.

6. Read Romans 8:11 and know that God has arranged for us to have an exciting and energized life. Dr. Lambert stated: "Eternal life is more than everlasting survival". Christ Himself, said that He came to give us abundant life. Consider that we must relinquish our own will on a daily basis to have this blessing. Make a promise to God now that you will surrender yourself to be obedient.

5

THE MYSTERY OF THE SEVEN ONES OF GOD

I therefore, the prisoner of the Lord, beseech you that ye walk worthy of the vocation wherewith ye are called, With all lowliness and meekness, with longsuffering, forbearing one another in love; Endeavoring to keep the unity of the Spirit in the bond of peace. There is one body, and one Spirit, even as ye are called in one hope of your calling; One Lord, one faith, one baptism, One God and Father of all, who is above all, and through all, and in you all. (Ephesians 4:1-6)

1. One Body
2. One Spirit - God the Spirit
3. One Hope
4. One Lord – God the Son
5. One Baptism
6. One Faith
7. One Father – God the Father

There are seven great mysteries. There are seven ones. There is but one of each of these sevens. We shall make the discovery that each one pertains to God's Person. Each of these sevens is of the nature of a miracle.

The idea behind each of these one is like unto our term, first. First in importance, first in power: Single in kind - one only. Preceding all others, it is foremost.

We shall see how these seven ones are each a wonder, a marvel, and a deviation from known laws, transcending man's knowledge. One is God's number, not man's! Satan thought he should be first. Many have adopted his line of thinking.

Seven signifies Completion

This unit of seven ones is the key to the entire New Testament. These literally interpret themselves. Reading from bottom to top, of the list of seven ones, on the opposite page, we discover three of these ones refer directly to the Holy Trinity; God the Father, God the Son, and God the Holy Spirit.

Since three, God's number of the Trinity denoting perfection and unity, pertains directly to Himself; would not this, then, be the immediate key to the whole passage? (The key to the door hangs near the entrance). In other words each of these sevens refers to our God, and not to the symbol or emblem. We, no doubt, will discover that although there is only one each, of these seven; yet there are many pictures, illustrations, and symbols.

One Father

Does not the passage declare there is One Father? Yet on this earth are many proud "Male Parents." There, are, it may be, many Dads, but only one Father. "But to us there is out one God, the Father, of whom are all things and we in Him; and one Lord Jesus Christ, by whom are all things, and we by Him." (1 Corinthians 8:6). There is but one Father God. All others are types, pictures, illustrations or imitations (?) perhaps.

One Lord

Although there may be many so called landlords across the country: perhaps numerous dukes sirs, and lords in the British Empire; yet there is no doubt, that all will agree that these are but little imitations of the Bible's One Lord, who is our wonderful Lord and Savior Jesus the Christ.

One Spirit

Would any fail to yield to the plain inference that the one Spirit is God the Holy Spirit? However you may recall the occasion where the legion of evil spirits were cast out of one man; yet these were lesser spirits, evil spirits. There is but one supreme Spirit; He is God; all others are lesser spirits.

The Mystery of the one Body; There is no Comparison, it is Supreme!

The unveiling of this superlative mystery will reveal an astounding creative act, even more stupendous than the act of causing nothingness to produce and bring forth a Mighty Universe. What, you ask, could be superior to the dramatic production of a vast system of worlds, out of the raw materials of nothingness? But! This one body is first and last. It is another and even greater creation, nothing like it, indeed cannot be, for it is the only one!

A Body Thou Hast Prepared in the Womb and the Tomb

"And the angel answered and said unto her, the Holy Ghost shall come upon thee, and the power of the Highest shall over-shadow thee: therefore also that holy thing which shall be born of thee shall be called the Son of God" (Luke 1:35). Mary did not bring Jesus Christ into existence. He lived in Heaven before He was born of Mary. God, through Mary's womb, brought into existence that Holy Thing. But! What was that Holy Things? Was it not His body? "A body thou hast prepared Me" (See Hebrews 10:5)

God's Redemption Plan Required A Miraculous One Body

Redemption's plan required a One Body prepared in the Virgin's womb as well as the tomb. "By the will we are sanctified through the offering of the body of Jesus Christ once for all" (Hebrews 10:10). That body, dear Christian, was prepared of God for the supreme sacrifice; offered of Him, on the cross for all.

Prepared in the womb of Mary, and glorified in the tomb; His terrestrial body merged with His eternal celestial self: Thus creative power has forged an extremely excellent body, suitable for the Supreme Being of the Universe.

Most Superior Miracle

Now for a superior miracle! His physical body, having been prepared in the womb of Mary was later eternalized, made omnipresence, and trans-materialized in the tomb. His made-glorious body became an essential part of Him. Your body is a part of you, even as His resurrected miracle body is a very part of Him.

A Visit to the Empty Tomb Revealed a Miraculous Body

The empty tomb received two excited inspectors that first Lord's Day. Following the most momentous sequence of events in history, the tomb revealed its powerless-ness to hold the One "Who God hath raised up, having loosed the pains of death: Because it was not possible that He should be holden of it" (Acts 2:24).

Peter, the sharp, and John the gentle, stepped into the sepulcher keenly desirous of ascertaining the true facts. Their startled eyes fell upon a glorious and spine tingling sight: Grave clothes - recently occupied. But, undisturbed! This was new! Nothing like it! The linen clothes lay precisely as when swathed round and around His crucified body. The Lord had passed through them. He needed not to be loosed as in the case of Lazarus. The Spirit had merged with the physical. In the power of resurrection He had been changed from the dead crucified One to the glorified body of Christ!

The solid rock wall of the tomb admitted free passage of the now tran-solidi (pass through solids) body of our death conquering Lord.

He has now made His triumphal entry into death's realm, and victorious exit from the tomb!

A Physical body Suitable for Heaven and Earth

Unlimited power fashioned a supreme body in keeping with the requirements of Deity's exalted rank and attributes. One of His attributes being omnipresence, His body must also be rendered omnipresence in order that He "May be all and in all."

The Supreme - Being of the Universe must possess a supreme body, in order that He may be trans-universal. Hence, one body! One First! His one body being preeminently first! The One at the top and head of the Universe has now a superior physical Body capable of super-human, supernatural, and even super-spiritual attainments.

This One-Body above and beyond physics, is not explainable on physical principles, because it is beyond and above earthly quality. Yet, it is a Body of "Flesh and bones" as per His entrance into the Upper Room, through the solid wall, also His passing through the grave clothes. This was a holy display of His physical-spiritual-body.

The Anointed One is Omnipresent, so is His Body

"At that day ye shall know that I am in My Father, and ye in Me and I in you." (John 14:20). Even as Jesus our Lord is omnipresent, so is His one body. The Body of Christ is capable of being superimposed upon and in every human body of every Christian on earth. The creation and glorification of Jesus' miraculous body is the acme of the majestic creative acts of an Almighty God.

Your passport to Distant Celestial Lands

This tremendous truth of Deity's one body inspires our awe as well as humbles our mind, as we contemplate its stupendous and eternal implications. The Supreme Being of this Universe has now a flesh and bones body capable of super human attainments; capable of being in all, over all, and through all; capable of being super-imposed upon every born again child of God.

Even as Christ is eternal, so His body is eternal. To be in Christ is to be in His eternal flesh and bones body. Glory! Even as Christ is omnipresent, so His body is capable of being omnipresent; upon and in every believer.

Heaven's Standard of Righteousness is Perfection

As Jesus Christ our Lord is perfect, so His plan is to perfect those who trust Him. He clothes His perfect self upon us; thus it is now possible for you, "That were sometime alienated and enemies in your mind by wicked works, yet now hath He reconciled in the body of His flesh through death, to present you holy and unblameable and unreprovable in His sight." (Colossians 1:21-22)

"Whom we preach, warning every man, and teaching every man in all wisdom: that we may present every man perfect in Christ Jesus." (Colossians 1:28).

We Have Met Heaven's Perfect Standard Perfectly

Your heavenly garment of perfection is Christ Jesus clothing Himself upon you. Thus, in Christ you are presented perfect; meeting Heaven's standard of righteousness perfectly. This is supernal love manifested in a most superior manner.

Since You Yield Your Body to Him Down Here; He Gives us a Body to Dwell in Up There

Our Dear Savior has found a way whereby He can go to the foreign field, as well as the home field. How? In us! By yielding our bodies to Him, the Savior may go to any field, in each of us, as He directs. Glory! What a franchise! One day we will undress from our present earthy body. The next day loved ones and friends will be saying, "He died last night". But! The truth of the matter will be, we will be walking the streets of glory. In what body? In our Christ given body "Not made with hands." Yes, in the glorious omnipresent body of Christ. In Christ, you will dwell in an eternal heavenly glorified body!

The Church Should Picture, Proclaim, Visualize and Even Portray this One Body; It should Never Claim to Be That One Body.

The flesh and bones body of Christ, far from being the Church is His own personal body, Christ Himself! "Therefore if any man be in Christ, he is a new creature: old things are passed away; behold all things are become new." (2 Corinthians 3:17). "For we are members of His body, (lest any imagine this to be the church body, allow the rest of the verse to interpret the first) of His flesh and of His bones" (Ephesians 5:30). These are the Spirit's own words.

What Does It Mean to Be In Christ?

Are we, as participants of the Mystery of the Ages, not clothed upon by His very presence? Are we to believe this is but a beautiful but metaphorical figuration? This, doubtless, would be an unbeliever's explanation. Jesus is a gracious and wonderful Person to be received. Are we not in Him? "As ye therefore received Christ Jesus the Lord, so walk ye in Him." (Colossians 2:6).

I Want All That's A'Coming to Me

In the words of a sharp little Chorus, "I want all that's a'comin to me, um, and a little bit, um, and a little bit, um, and a whole lot more."

Secure Full Value

In order to secure all that's a coming to you, obey three simple rules:

1. Read all that the Bible has to say on any given subject or doctrine.
2. Compare Scripture with Scripture. The Bible is the Holy Spirit's own commentary. The Bible will explain the Bible and interpret it.

3. Believe every word. Understand the meaning of each word in accordance with Bible usage, and not outside Bible meanings.

Mystery of the Bible Explained

The Holy Spirit dictated a letter to the Colossian Christians. This epistle declares the Mystery of the Ages revealed in these last days. How? Through the mind of some great theologian? Indeed no, but, from the pages of Holy Writ. God's Revelation!

By following our three simple rules we shall now take the much controverted term "body" and discover to our startled minds that this method of Bible study will unfold a so astonishing truth as to leave some trembling with joy. Others may tremble with rage. I believe it is the Holy Spirit who registers joy in our hearts. It is Satan who stirs up anger. The Word of God will make one mad or glad.

One Body, Not Many, Not Even Two

The Spirit-Teacher is most explicit in His authoritative statement in His Ephesians' dictation that there is one body. Now! Beloved, if there is but one body, whose is it? Would one dare say that a church body of believers has the preeminence over the personal, glorious flesh and bones body of Christ?

Certify the Bible's Own Usage of the Term One

The idea of this one is like unto the term first. First in importance (none greater) Amen! Single in kind - foremost - preceding all others, etc. May we learn a lesson from the Prince of Demons! Satan thought he should be first.

The Church, even if it were a worldwide thing, since it is made up of people (earth dwellers), could never supersede Christ. Could a body of people, no matter how important, ever be superior to Jesus Christ? Why should any wish to lower our Savior and supplant Him with another? Would not a Universal Church Body displace His

Body, that is, if it referred to this "One Body?" Since there-is but one body - one first-one greatest, how could this refer to the Church without lowering Jesus Christ?

One is God's Number, Not Man's

Christ's holy and glorious flesh and bones body is as much Christ as your body is you. It is His humanity part! Is not His resurrection body, now, a very part of His eternal Self? Could any deny the following two verses are synonymous? "If any man be in Christ . . ." (2 Corinthians 5:17). "We are members of His body, of His flesh, and of His bones" (See Ephesians 5:30).

Hath Made Both One

By the operation of the New Birth, God's sinless, spotless, holy Son, and the saved sinner are fused (meaning to unite or blend, as melted together); thus He is in you, and you, in Him (see John 14:20).

"That He might reconcile both unto God in One Body by the cross, having slain the enmity thereby" (Ephesians 2:16). Is this one body the Church? Is it the "Mystical Body" (?) (a man-made term)? If so, we are forced to the ridiculous conclusion that it was this mystical body which hanged on the cross; "slew the enmity thereby, "and reconciled all, whether Jew or Gentile. Yet the Bible explains "Having abolished in His flesh the enmity . . .; for to make (create) in Himself of twain (two) one new man (New Creature) so making peace." (Ephesians 2:15).

You and Christ: A New Man

"If any man be in Christ, he is a new creature." That new creation, then, is "you in Christ and Christ in you". You and Christ are now one new man. "For He is our peace who hath made (created) both one." Amen! (See Ephesians 2:14)

One Must Not Only Obey the Law of Context But Also Compare Scripture with Scripture.

By comparing Bible terms and words, carefully considering their Holy Spirit usage, the Scriptures will discover for you the intended meaning of a passage. Some present day ministers have a satchel full of expositions on the matter; all worthy enough to be read in a dark room. If and since you and Christ are a new creation in 2 Corinthians 5:17, why profane the Scriptures by manmade interpretation, and make "one new man" mean something else in the book of Ephesians?

Is it not-in His crucified flesh and bone Body that He makes "in" Himself of twain one new man? Do Holy Spirit terms have reference to one thing in one portion of His Book, and something else elsewhere? Our Savior's own method is to search the Scriptures. Should I seek the services of Dr. Spoof, Pastor Hatcherown, Rev. I. Tickle Ears, Radio Speaker J. Fuller Dryasdust, or even the Right Rev. Sol Hotaire? Since these dear gentlemen do not agree among themselves, I hardly know which Doctor to call.

Did not our God give us the very words He wished used? In the case of Jeremiah He put those words in his mouth. Are we to believe the good Lord actually put words in a prophet's mouth? Are we honestly to believe that little donkey spoke? Yes, indeed! We may even know the language used. Perhaps, it was He-Bray!

One Body; Many Pictures
Consider: One Body, many pictures. Each local church should picture to its community Christ's one body. Although one is compelled to confess that there are some mighty poor likenesses about these days of apostasy. Is not this principle of the one of universal usage, as well as maintained throughout the Scriptures? Note:

The Principle of the One

1. The Bible, many copies.
2. One Lamb of God, but many lambs.
3. One Father, many male parents.
4. One Baptism, many pictures.
5. One Body of Christ, many local churches.
6. One Spirit, many angelic spirits.

7. One Lord, many land-lords.
8. One Christ, many anti-christs.
9. One you, Dear Reader, but perhaps, many pictures.

The New Man verses the Old Man
"Lie not one to another, seeing that ye nave put off the old man with his deeds; and have put on the new man . . ." (Colossians 3:9-10). Is this new man the church? Just how would one go about putting on the church? Again, in the Book of Ephesians, we are told to put off the old man and put on the new. "For in Christ Jesus neither circumcision availeth anything, nor uncircumcision, but a new creature" (Galatians 6:15).

What is the Body of Christ?
Many conflicting beliefs are being propagated, today, as to what constitutes the Body of Christ. May we set before us several of the most widely taught theories of the day?

Many believe the Body of Christ constitutes the sum total of all born-again believers.   Others reckon this to mean their particular denomination. Another belief is that this one body refers to the local church. Still others hold that, Body of Christ is synonymous with the Bride of Christ. Yet many more maintain that the One Body refers to the Mystical Body or True Church.

Peter, Peter Pumpkin Eater
The teacher of a Sunday School Class asked little Girty if she could remember any of the details concerning their previous lessons on the Apostle Peter. Girty allowed she could tell a couple of things on him. The bright little one was asked to proceed. "Well," said Girty, "For one thing he had trouble with his wife; and another thing, he liked pumpkins." "Oh!" Cried the astonished Sunday School Instructor, "Where did you get that information?" Girty's reply was, "I can quote the verse." "Please do, then," urged the bewildered one." "Here goes,"

quoted Girty: "Peter, Peter, Pumpkin eater; Had a wife, but, couldn't keep her!" Well, perhaps, we must learn to ascertain between nursery rhyme and the Holy Scriptures.

Which Body?

May we list several verses in which the term body appears? By obeying the Law of Context I feel quite sure our hearts may well be startled to learn the Bible's Builder refers to three different bodies in one Book. The three bodies are: Human Body - Church Body - Christ's body.

1. The human body: "Putting off the body of the sins of the flesh." (Colossians 2:11).
2. The church Body: "And He is the head of the body the Church." (Colossians. 1:18).
3. Christ's flesh and bones body: "In the body of His flesh" (Colossians 1:22).

Three Bodies in Ephesians

Human Body - Men ought to love their wives as own bodies (5:28).

Church Body - To the Church which is His body (1:22-23).

His Flesh and Bone Body - "We are members of His Body of His flesh and of His bones" (5:30).

Allow the Holy Spirit to define and interpret the exact meaning of the word, "Body" as it appears in any particular text. Each passage will display, by the context and related passages, the sought for sense and meaning. These verses exhibit the fact that the Epistles are God's own commentary!

Also, His Post Resurrection body

Some Scripture passages refer to the Human Body; the Church Body is being considered in others; yet again the subject is Jesus' Flesh and

Bones Body; but, still again, the Post Resurrection Body of our glorified Savior is the theme.

The Holy Spirit's Explicit Statement: There is One Body!

Christ's glorious flesh and bone body; The Church Body; The human body. Which of the above three would the angels declare to be that one body? In the Father's presence, which one would you choose to be the one body of Christ? The "Flesh and Bones Body" of Christ should never be wrested to mean the Church Body. To do so is to rob our Lord of honor and prestige. To misappropriate these terms is to cheat His blood bought ones of the glorious truth concerning this miracle body, which the church body should picture.

You are respectfully urged to gather into one group all the verses which are often used to teach a one church (Universal Church) theory, and examine each in the light of the context. Compare Scripture with Scripture, allow each word to mean exactly what it says, ignore outside the Bible-text interpretations, and discover the startling fact that these very verses refer, not to a church body, but, rather, to His own personal flesh and bones body that carne forth from the tomb.

Redemption's Plan Required An Exclusive One Body

First - Salvation's plan required a "One Body" so preeminently exclusive as to debar all others. It must be the holiest of holies. It must be Restricted to One. It is to be God's Body! It is to be suitable for both Heaven's Holy City and earth as well. Unlike man's inherited sinful body; God's must be holy to the extreme. It is to be set apart for worship. It is a very part of Him! It is to be hallowed and adored of angels.

Second - His body must be suitable for redemption's purposes! Placed in the scale of values, His one body is exceedingly superior to all others. He is of greater value than all others combined. All others, even in their accumulative value, are of lesser worth. His Body must be of exceeding greater value than all others combined. IT is to be the ransom for these! It is limited to "one body" by virtue of the fact this, God's Body, must be as brilliantly distinguished above all others combined; as light in respect to darkness.

Third – must be begotten of God. His body must be sacred and holy in its conception. Unlike man's body which was "conceived in sin," Christ's must be the result of a special, never to be performed again, miracle. It is to become a very part of God!

Fourth – It is God's Body to be Indwelt by the Holy Trinity. Man's natural body is limited to the housing of one person or soul. God's Body is to be indwelt by three Persons; the Father, the Son, and the Holy Ghost. This One Body is "Prepared" in the virgin's womb and further glorified in Calvary's tomb. We are not to imagine this One Body limits Deity's attributes or senses; therefore, we must consider it as being competent of rendering His attributes and senses trans-universal.

The body capable of housing the three Persons of the God-Head, must not limit, but allow Him to see and hear and feel, across the universe! Each local church, as well as each individual in that church, should be devoted to the task of proclaiming to their community, this One who's Body is so exclusive and so transcendently holy as to allow the God-Head to actually take up their residence there!

Both Human and Divine
His human body has been deified by a grand creative act of Deity Himself. "Therefore also that holy thing which shall be born of thee shall be called the Son of God" (Luke 1:35).

One Body so Elevated in Worth and Exchange Value as to be in Excess of the Total inflated value of all mankind.
Our Savior must not only give His Body as an excessively rich price, far above the appraised value of the entire human race, but, He must absolve, exonerate, and vindicate, as well as pardon, each sinner who petitions Him for salvation. He clears from guilt, each of these, in order

that He may also acquit them. Speaking of purchasing power, enough of the purchase price has been credited to our account in Heaven, to redeem you and the whole human race. Praise be His forever!

The Word was Made Flesh!
The union of Divinity with humanity, in Jesus Christ, has bestowed on the world an endowment as a permanent love fund. Who are the designated beneficiaries? Are they not the sinners who in faith call upon God for pardon?

Christ is All and in All
"Christ is all, and in all." Does not this statement, of Colossians 3:11 leave one in a state of overwhelming wonder? Is it possible for the Spirit Teacher to reveal so tremendous a mystery to our finite minds? How could Christ be all, and in all? Recall, amazed Reader, two God given words: First - the word spirit. Second - the word one. One is God's number.

"For there is one God and one Mediator between God and man, the Man Christ Jesus." There is one God, one only. Yet we know there are three persons in one God. Three separate and distinct Persons are in the Godhead. Now! Jesus makes this astonishing request: "Holy Father, Keep through Thine own name those whom Thou hast given Me, that they (many) may be one, as We are." (John 17:21-23).

Spiritual Block Buster
Startling! Mysterious! Shocking! None the less it is true. Even as a legion (upwards of 4000) evil spirits could be one in the body of a man; so Jesus prays that all His Calvary bought ones should be one in Him. Our Teacher will further enlighten us if we will but listen to His continuing prayer: "As they all may be one; as Thou, Father, art in Me, and I in Thee, that they also may be one in us . . . (does not say, all one in the church). And the glory which Thou hast given Me I have given them; that they

may be one even as We are one; I in them, and Thou in Me, that they may be made perfect in one." (John 17:11, 21-23). Praise Him!

A Christian is a Spirit

"That which is born of the Spirit is Spirit." (John 3:6). In the spirit-realm, material things, such as walls, grave clothes, flesh, and solids, can neither bar nor limit a spirit being. You and all born of the Spirit ones are spirit beings. Thus, as many evil spirits could indwell one man, so all born of the Spirit - spirits can and do dwell in Christ's one flesh and bones body.

"For ye are all one in Christ Jesus." (Galatians 3:28). The same God used principle as makes three Persons in One, is now used to make millions of persons one. As three Persons can be in one, so 4000 could be in one, or for that matter, even millions. Hence, "For ye are all one in Christ Jesus."

Prepared in the Womb and Glorified in the Tomb

Jesus' body was prepared in the Virgin's womb for crucifixion, it was glorified, and eternized, omni-presentized, made tran-solidi, and trans-universalized in the tomb. Hence, the Father, in Jesus Christ's one body is "In all, through (fused in all) all and above all." (Ephesians 4:6).

Christ is All and in All

Reverse the above Bible Statement and you have its interpretation. If Christ is in Tom, Dick, and Harriet, then He has become Tom with Tom, Dick with Dick, and Harriet with Harriet. Thus He is all three. In like manner: if Christ is in all, then it just naturally follows He is all. "Christ is all and in all." (Colossians 3:11).

"Ye are all one in Christ Jesus." (Gal. 3:28). If Tom, Dick and Harriet are in Christ Jesus; by virtue of those facts, they are all three, one in Him. Glory! Thus, Jesus' prayer statement in John 17:22: "And the glory which Thou gavest Me I have given them; that they (being many) may be one, even (this is the explanation) as We (the Godhead) are one." Oh! What a glory!

A Bride of His Flesh and Bones

Down here all Christians are in His One resurrected and glorified flesh and bones body. He is even now gathering all in Heaven and on earth into one; even Him. "That in the dispensation of the fullness of times He might gather together in one all things in Christ, both which are in Heaven, and which are on earth: even in Him." (Ephesians 1:10). In this manner He becomes "all and in all."

In Heaven, after the rapture, each crucified member of His One Body will become an integral part of the Bride of Christ. Thus, the Last Adam will have a Bride of "His flesh and His bones." (Eph. 5:30). Should we not remember, there is no bride until there is a wedding? Praise God! There is to be a wedding in the sky!

Study, Discussion & Application Points for Chapter 5

1. Read and study this chapter.
2. The key verse for this chapter is 2 Corinthians 5:17: *"Therefore if any man be in Christ, he is a new creature: old things are passed away; behold, all things are become new."*
3. The great Christmas announcement is made to Mary in Luke 1:35. The angel told Mary she would host the development of the "holy one". We know that Mary did not bring God, the Son into existence. Other passages clearly teach that He lived in eternity past and was the Creator of all. However, God saw fit that Jesus would need an earthly body in order to relate and communicate His love to the human race. Look at these verses and write down your thoughts about the necessity of Christ's earthly body:
   - Hebrews 10:5
   - Colossians 1:19-22

4. Dr. Lambert explains that Christ's body was changed in the tomb. The resurrected body of Christ would prove to be "capable of super-human, supernatural, and even super-spiritual attainments". The resurrected Jesus was able to pass through grave clothes and closed doors and even instantly travel between heaven and earth. Yet, it is very clear that Christ maintained His "flesh and blood" body. Note these verses:
   • Luke 24:39
   • John 21:12-13

5. Just as God prepared a new body for Christ, He also has in mind a new body for every believer. The Apostle said in 1 Corinthians 15:51 "We shall not all sleep (die), but we shall all be changed" meaning those caught up in the Lord's rapture will also instantly be "re-made" with a body like Christ's resurrected body. Note the following passages and write down your thoughts:
   • 1 Corinthians 15:43-53
   • Philippians 3:20-21

6. Jesus Christ, in His human body, became familiar with the troubles, limitations and even temptations that all people face. He truly understands every physical and emotional struggle that we face. Look at the following verses to determine the exclusiveness and extent of Christ's ministry.
   • Hebrews 10:10
   • Hebrews 4:14-16

6

THE MYSTERY OF ONE BAPTISM

Mystery surrounds the very term baptism. The entire realm of Gospel Truths is packaged in one word: Baptism!

Mystery surrounds the very term baptism. Beyond the Bible's own revelation it remains a profound secret. It defies and baffles all attempts to explain. When so called scholars and ambitious denominational leaders make a mad scramble to expound this enigma, the total result is a mad scramble. We may quickly locate the crux of this perplexing problem by comparing two seemingly contradictory verses of Scripture. Although one apparently negates the other, yet, these are only ostensibly contrary; since Bible verses do not oppose one another.

Note these Bible References:

> One - "One baptism" - singular (Ephesians 4:5).
> Two - "Doctrine of baptisms" - plural (Hebrews 6:2).

Thus our mystery is further complicated by this; the bewildering assertion that there is but one baptism. Since other Bible verses speak of baptisms (plural), how are we to understand this apparent contradiction? Is there really just one baptism, or are there many? It would appear, then, we may be in the midst of a dilemma (two horns).

First horn - One baptism (singular).

Second horn - Doctrine of baptisms (plural).

Hornswoggle and Bamboozle

Old Hornie (Scat for devil) would like to hornswoggle (meaning to bamboozle) the honest student of the Word into believing the Bible is full of contradictions, and is only a man inspired hoax. There are too many around, already, who are sneer sighted.

The purpose of this area of the book is to paint to the fact that the Spirit-Teacher has a thrilling and happy solution to this complicated mystery. Will you prepare your good heart for this anticipated soul satisfying surprise?

The Whole Gospel Message is Packaged in This One Word: Baptism

The entire realm of Gospel truths is wrapped up in this one word, baptism. The meaning of this term, baptism, is to be deduced from its usage, Holy Spirit usage, Bible usage; not its original pristine sense alone, neither its origin, nor its significance as employed by the Greeks; but by God's intended meaning of the word as disclosed in His Book; by comparing Scripture with Scripture.

Don't dig up some dead Greek, and ask Him what God means by the word "Baptizo," for it is a converted word, a God changed word; it is a God appropriated word, made over and sanctified. Employed of God, baptize is a word with a new import, a brand new word. It is a vehicle of thought, with a deeper meaning which symbolizes the whole Gospel story. The total Gospel message is packaged in this term, "One Baptism."

Baptism Does Not Always Mean Immersion in Water

God has made the term, "One Baptism," serve to express, or convey, a mental image of Calvary's scenes. It describes the three momentous happenings of the main episode of His Son's mission in the world. In God's adaptation of the Word, He has fitted it to mean the threefold event called Calvary:

First - Death of that One Body
Second - Burial of that One Body
Third - Resurrection of that One Body.

Our Father has applied the term, "One Baptism," to His Son's crucifixion, burial, and resurrection; hence, one baptism - one first one
supreme, none other like it or equal to it. This is the Father' s own
Son' s death, burial and resurrection - elevated and preeminently
above all others. There is never to be another like it - could not be -
because this is to be God's own death, and burial, and resurrection.
This term one baptism could be applied to but One person; the One
who is first; the One who is entitled to preeminence – Our Lord Jesus
Christ!

Calvary Baptism

Jesus' one baptism is devoted to redemption. He, Himself, taught His
followers, "Ye shall be baptized with the baptism I am baptized with"
(See Matthew 20:22-23). His baptism is the original; the "one first".
All others pictures, figures, portrayals, and examples are of that one
baptism. These other "baptisms" (Hebrews 6:2) are marvelous, acted
out pictures or patterns of that original and only one real baptism!

Jordan Baptism

Jesus spoke of a post Jordan baptism: "But I have a baptism to be
baptized with, and how am I straitened till it be accomplished" (Luke
12:50). "Jesus answered and said, "Ye know not what ye ask. Are ye
able to drink of the cup that I shall (future) drink of, and to be (future) baptized with the baptism that I am baptized with?" They say
unto Him, "We are able." And He saith unto them, "Ye shall (future)
drink indeed of my cup, and be (future) baptized with the baptism
that I am baptized with ..." (Matthew 20:22-23).

Addressing a Bible class on the above subject I inquired of my
hearers, What baptism was Jesus talking about? A house wife replied
with this, "Why, was He not speaking of His Jordan Baptism?" "But,"

I reminded this good woman, "He has already been baptized in the River Jordan, according to Matthew Chapter Three. Yet, He is speaking of a future baptism for Himself and His followers."

Another class member, a nurse, suggested, "Perhaps He was speaking of His anointing of the Spirit, as a baptism." Again I reminded my interested class that the Holy Spirit came upon the Lord immediately-following His Jordan Baptism.

Have not the apostles, also, been immersed in water? Yet, He declares, they too are to be baptized with Him. "And He saith unto them, ye shall drink indeed of my cup, and be baptized with the Baptism I am baptized with." "Ye shall... indeed... be baptized with the baptism that I am baptized with."

Please Consider Two Propositions
First: Every born again believer is saved from the penalty and - power of sin on the basis of Jesus' death, burial, and resurrection. Second: The born again one is in Christ.

How Does One Enter Into Christ?
We know the Holy Spirit can take a surrendered sinner, turn him into a New Creature by putting that one into Christ. But! By what operation does God advance a sinner from his lost estate into the Savior's Body? How does the Spirit dwell the believer in Christ?

Most Astonishing Answer
"For as many of you as have been baptized into Christ have put on Christ" (Galatians 3:27). Remember, Jesus said, "Ye shall...indeed be baptized with the baptism I am baptized with". The Spirit tells us, "Wherefore if ye be dead with Christ ..." What was the cause of this death? Sin, of course. But, what was the mode of death? The Spirit through Paul's pen answers our question: "I am crucified with

Christ..." (Galatians 2:20). What was the instrument of that death? Does not crucifixion mean death on the cross?

These Verses Meet at the Crossroads

All these verses, and many more to follow, are simply the affirmation and explanation as well as confirmation of Jesus' prophetic assertion, "Ye shall be baptized with the baptism (same one baptism) that I am baptized with."

Now Observe This Wonderful Verse Unfold as We Understand it to be the Fulfillment of Our Dear Savior's Prophecy Concerning the Believer's Calvary-Baptism

"Know ye not, that so many of us as were baptized into Jesus Christ (notice: enter into - Jesus Christ by baptism), were baptized into His death (now, does not the blessed Spirit tell us, plainly, we are baptized into His death?). Was not His death by crucifixion? Is this not Calvary-Baptism?

"Therefore we (many) are buried with Him (how?) by baptism into death (Well! Here we are in the dark, damp, tomb. But! We are not alone. He is with us. While down here in the sepulcher, let us make an eternal decision. May we promise God we will never again live the same old life - after our emergence from this tomb.

We will walk in newness of life, which like as Christ was raised up from the dead. Now, while here in the tomb, let us observe the tremendous operation of God as He actually raises His own dead Son! This carefully formulated plan of resurrection is called an "operation" in the Colossian Epistle, chapter two, and verse twelve. While in this Roman's passage it is called "glory".

Peer intently toward the hinder part of the tomb, where the body of His Son rests upon the bier. Now! Observe! Jesus approaches the bier after His emergence from the "Heart of the earth." Watch! He re-enters His body; the Spirit melts into the flesh. The physical is fused with the spiritual.

By a stupendous miracle, the Heavenly Father, glorifies His Son by making His body "Tran-solidi" (pass through solids). Immediately thereafter, Jesus transfers His body through the grave clothes, as the Spirit of the Father-Himself, enters into the now glorified body of His death conquering Son.

The Dear Father's Own Definition and Interpretation and Exposition of His Term "One Baptism"

Now, consider please: "That like as Christ was raised up from the dead by the glory of the Father, even so we also should walk in Newness of life (See Romans 6:1-4). Even as Christ was changed and glorified by the Father, even so, we too, here in the tomb, with Him, are being made new by this same tremendous power.

By an astonishing miracle Jesus enters into your body! Marvelous! Hallelujah! This miraculous operation is fitted to excite wonder and admiration. Even the angel throngs press forward to observe and marvel! Angelic hosts are struck with surprise at this new thing. A new creation! You and Christ, astonished Christian, are that "New Creation"!

By a tremendous miracle Jesus enters into your body. This is in answer to His prayer plea, "I in them, and Thou in me, that they may be perfect in One" (John 17:23). Here is His own startling explanation: "As Thou, Father, art in Me, and I in Thee that they also may be one in Us."

Christ in You; The Hope of Glory

Child of God, this is salvation! God's own redemption plan – Christ in you, the hope of glory. The one word that expresses the process is baptism! This is, now, a word full of meaning - designed (redesigned) to describe or give an account of the operation by which a sinner is turned into a saint.

The Holy Spirit Emphasizes the Preposition "With"

Jesus taught His followers that they would be baptized *with* His baptism. Please note the frequency of the appearance of the preposition *with*. It is used often, of the Spirit in connection with our term baptism.

Entombed with Christ

"Buried with Him in baptism, Glory! Here we are buried with Him, in His tomb. Beloved! Will you dare to believe, while here in the dark tomb with Him, the tremendous truth of all that is now transpiring, as we, for a short fleeting moment, remain here buried with our Savior?

We are "Putting off the old man - putting on the new man." We are, here, becoming a new creature - a new creation. The old man is passing away. We are "putting off the body of the sins of the flesh". "Wherein (during the course of - that is while in the tomb) also ye are risen with Him (now we are being resurrected with Him) through the faith of the operation of God (by the exceeding greatness of His power to us-ward...which He wrought in Christ, when He raised Him from the dead... beloved, this is our conversion.) Converted from a lost sinner into a saint of God, by the mighty power of our Lord.

The same operation that raised Jesus from the dead, also resurrects us with Him. Only Almighty God could perform the miracle of eliminating the time element, reach across the centuries, and appropriate this same baptism to believers today. Glory! In fact this is the same resurrection that resurrected Christ; as per the following, "Who hath raised Him from the dead ... quickened together with Him (Colossians 2:11-13). God's act of forgiveness takes place while we are in the tomb with His Son. The old man is put to death, passes away, and the new man is ready to live on the resurrection side of the tomb." Quickened together with Him.

The Bible's Own Concept of Baptism

The authority for this Scriptural concept may be affirmed by its perfect agreement and conformity with every other passage. I must admit it does not agree with many man-made commentaries or teachings on the subject. But, all other Bible verses (God's Commentaries) consent to this view; even correlating and harmonizing in perfect accord.

One Baptism of That One Body
God has made one baptism to mean:

> First - Death of that one body.
> Second - Burial of that one body.
> Third - Resurrection and glorification of that one body.

Wrapped up in this God appropriated, and now converted, descriptive term one baptism are the miracles of redemption; even the New Birth itself. The power of this one baptism is tremendous. It slays, buries, and resurrects each individual, the instant one yields to God for salvation. No other baptism could do this!

An Old Word Converted
In order to accomplish all this, the Father must prepare His Son a special physical body. That One Body must be crucified, buried, and glorified by a special resurrection. God must now find a word that signifies all this. But no word could be found among earth dweller's languages that would suit God's purpose. So and old word must be converted, changed, magnified, enlarged, and even glorified.

Beware: Hoof-Prints of Satan
Converted Words, like converted people will at times backslide
Our Lord's vicious enemy, Satan, has corrupted the word baptism; causing some to embrace the picture, rather than the One pictured. By marring the picture, the devil has disfigured the concept. What is the purpose or function of a picture? Is it not to figure forth or represent visibly the person or thing portrayed? A defaced image obstructs the purpose of showing what the real thing looks like.

The real thing to be pictured, in this case, is the crucifixion, entombment, and glorious resurrection of our Redeemer and Lord. Bible usage has converted the word baptism and made it mean, or signify, the one death, burial and resurrection of God. Baptism (God's death, burial, and resurrection) is the process by which God produces a Christian (Christ-in-one) out of the raw material called a sinner.

A Misnomer (incorrect designation) or Define Your Terms Please: Baptism Does Not Always Mean Immersion in Water

Biblically and technically speaking, immersion in water is not baptism. It is the picture or figure of that one baptism. Technically it would be incorrect to call the picture of a loved one, by that loved one's name. Though, colloquially, we very often do.

A group of folk in a Bible class, one afternoon, was amused when the speaker pointed to a picture on a nearby mantle, at the same time asking, "Who is that?" The hostess replied, "That is my sister, who resides in California." "You mean," he continued, smiling broadly, "Your sister actually lives in California; yet she sits each day upon your mantle? Why, that's nothing short of a miracle." The point was won amidst laughter!

When one marries, he does not marry and embrace the picture of his bride; but, rather, the real thing. One should embrace Calvary's one baptism of our Lord, and not water baptism which is its picture. Although each obedient new born Christian will certainly submit to beautiful water baptism.

One Bible... Many Copies! One Lamb... Many Types! One Baptism... Many Pictures!

A slip in terminology has caused many to jump the cog, and thus get off the track. That seemingly insignificant twist in the meaning of that word, baptism, has thrown Christendom a curve. In the words of a Baptist friend, "It has given us a bad-twist."

One Baptism! Although the Rite May be Performed Many Hundreds of Thousands of Times

The miraculous saving power of Jesus' Calvary Baptism (His death, burial, and resurrection) is applied to each sinner the moment he presents himself to God for salvation. The Holy Spirit applies that one baptism. Thus, "By One Spirit are we all baptized into one body..." (1 Corinthians 12:13). Is this not in perfect accord with, "As many of you as have been baptized into Christ, have put on Christ" (Galatians 3:27).

In other words, as many as have been crucified with Christ, buried with Christ, and resurrected with Christ are in (have put on Christ) Him. The word, baptism, is a term that quickly expresses all that took place at Calvary, in the tomb, the resurrection? Pentecost, as well as the meaning and purpose of those events.

When Were the Apostles and Immediate Followers of Christ Baptized with Jesus' Baptism?

When were the Apostles baptized with Jesus' Baptism? Were they not baptized the day the Holy Baptizer came to do His office work, as Administrator of Jesus estate and legacy? According to Jesus' last will and testament; He wills us His death, burial, resurrection, and His glorified body. The Spirit administers all these gifts to each believer on the day of their salvation. Bless God!

Calvary and Pentecost

In exact accordance with prophecy the Holy Spirit came on Pentecost Day to publicly appropriate to each one that which Jesus had willed them. He left to each one His risen glorified Body. Each one, by the Spirit, is crucified with Christ, buried with Christ, and risen with Christ. Thus, he is baptized with Jesus' baptism, in exact accordance with His own prophetic-promise.

Far from baptizing all believers into some supposed mystical body, the Holy Ghost baptized each individual into His bequeathed glorified body. If any man be in Christ, he is a new creature. Peter and the others went out and gave the world a demonstration of the fact they were new creatures. Today, it is still true, if any man be in Christ he is a new creation. This demonstration should be given to the world by each one whom thus walks in newness of life.

Christ's Glorified Body, Not the Church
If the new convert understands, as he should, that he is in Christ? That is, in His glorified body, he will go out and show the world he and Christ are now one. However, if he imagines that one body is an association of an invisible mystical body of believers; how can he understand the presence and power of the very Christ who he indwells? Does not one feel inclined, perhaps, to think that this is the cause of much powerlessness in Christians today?

Consternation Among the Angels
These verses, pertaining to the physical presence of Christ's own body, if used to represent a mystical church body, must cause consternation among the holy angels of God as they behold so majestic a truth lowered to a point less than the Highest. Honor the church body, love her, and serve God through her; but, never elevate her above her Lord. Let us not appropriate holy terms to her when those terms refer to her Lord!

Somebody Left the Gate Open
The misinterpretation of the terms, body of Christ and Baptism, opens the gate to a host of False Teachings, who seeing the gate wide open rush out to propagate themselves as genuine. Now consider these two top priority doctrines: one body and one baptism. If this one baptism constitutes Calvary baptism of our dear Savior, or in other words, His death, burial and resurrection, then immediately the gate is closed to all these false baptisms. Since it is the one baptism that took place at Calvary that saves the sinner (and not water

baptism), then water baptism is put in its rightful place by becoming a picture (figure) of the one baptism.

The One Body: Not a Denomination, But the Crucified Body of Our Redeemer

Some teach that the body or Christ is their denomination. They further instruct (obstruct) that all who wish to enter Heaven must come and allow their preachers to baptize them into their church. What an absurd assumption this becomes in the light of the truth that the one body far from being a church or denomination, is the actual "Flesh and Bones Body" of our Redeemer. It is the crucifixion of that precious prepared one body that saves the soul, not the joining of some church.

The One Baptism Rules Our a Baptism Subsequent to Salvation

The idea of a baptism after salvation is ruled out by the truth of a one baptism and one only. Although there is, most certainly, a time when the convert should make a complete surrender to their Lord. This may rightly be termed dedication. When God's child does yield unreservedly his body, soul, and spirit to the indwelling Christ, this will result in the appropriation of the power and glory of that one baptism. Hence the manifestation of Jesus' death and resurrection is made real in the consciousness of the believer. It may seem to that one that he has just been baptized into Christ; so real may become the power, the joy, and the peace, of the presence of the abiding Christ.

Actually all this was theirs from the time of their salvation. Calvary's Baptism was appropriated to them at the moment of conversion But, they did not, perhaps, cash in till weeks or months, or even years later. (The convert should submit to water baptism because it is a picture of the one). The fact of it was theirs from the second of salvation;   but, the reality of it did not become theirs until they met the conditions of full surrender.

Can We Rightly Call the Anointing of the Spirit a Baptism?

Upon the authority of the Scriptures there is but one baptism. Obviously, the one baptism being the death, burial, and resurrection of Jesus at Calvary. Can we correctly term the filling of the Spirit a baptism? Since baptism means a plunge, a burial, a resurrection, how could we ever rightly term the anointing of the Holy Spirit a baptism? Considering the fact that the Builder or the Bible does not so use these terms, would one not be a wrester of the Scriptures to thus misuse them?

What Baptism Does Not Mean

Should one resort to outside the Bible sources to ascertain the Spirit's meaning of a word, term, or passage? Should one not allow the Holy Bible's use of the word to determine its true meaning? Has not God so constructed the Bible as to permit it to thus explain itself?

Hence, the Bible does not explain that Jesus' post-Jordan Baptism simply means a "Flood of judgments,   afflictions, overwhelming trials, or visitations." Beloved, is that not just man's supposition, surmise, conjecture and crude guess work?

The Jordan Baptism of Jesus, as Well as That of His Disciples, was a prophetic Portrayal of His Own One Baptism at Calvary

The Holy Spirit cannot take you 1900 years back to Calvary, so He brings Calvary to you. You can, today, say with the Apostle Paul, "I am crucified with Christ." According to Jesus' own prophetic statement, each and all are "Baptized with the baptism that I am baptized with" (Matthew 20:23).

The Holy Spirit does not baptize with Water baptism; but with Calvary Baptism. On the Day of Pentecost the Spirit applied the miracle of Calvary's Baptism to the tarrying believers. Now, today, no believer needs tarry for the baptism. For the Holy Baptizer instantly baptizes the surrendering sinner with Jesus' one baptism, putting each one into Christ. "For by one Spirit are we all baptized into One Body..." (1 Corinthians 12:13).

Each water baptism, and all other baptisms such as, "And were all baptized unto Moses in the cloud and in the sea…" (1 Corinthians 10:2), are types and portrayals of Calvary's One Baptism of Christ.

Jesus Resigned His Position of Holiest Son

Think of it! That priceless one body battered, pierced, and fastened to two beams; one pointing toward Heaven, the other pointing across the universe, He resigned the position of the Holiest Son, to become the Criminal of the Universe. "For He hath made Him to be sin for us, who knew no sin, that we might be made the righteousness of God in Him" (1 Cor. 5:21).

Calvary Baptism is the process or operation by which God punishes the sinner's Savior; slays Him; and buries Him in order to resurrect a glorified body capable of dwelling in every believer, and dwelling every believer in Him. The Holy Administrator administers this operation to the surrendered sinner. This one baptism is the process of the New Birth. The Old Man is destroyed, and passes away, while a New Man is created and brought into existence.

"Knowing this, that our old man is crucified with Him, that the body of sin might be destroyed, that henceforth we should not serve sin…" (Romans 6:6). The Spirit must execute the body of sin by applying Jesus' death. He contributes the one body which has been eternalized, Tran-solidized and omnipresentized. Thus He tenders you the benefits of the resurrection by fusing Christ with you. By this grand operation the Holy Spirit, Who is the Baptizer, makes the believer and Christ "one" (John 17:23).

Why does our beloved Savior dwell Himself "In all?" Why does He so desire to dwell all believers in Himself? Why! In order that He "May be all and in all" (Colossians 3:11).

Those In Christ Should Be In His Church
If one is in His flesh and bones body, he should be desirous, also, to identify himself with God and His people by being in His church-body. "He is the Head of the body, the Church..." (Colossians 1:18).

When you accepted Christ, your friends did not see you crucified with Christ; neither did they see you buried in His tomb. Furthermore, they did not observe you being resurrected with your Savior. At the exact moment of salvation, you actually entered into Christ's glorified body. But, with the veil of flesh over natural eyes, they were unable to see this great transaction.

This is where water baptism and the church body play their important roll. Water Baptism pictures the operation of Calvary's baptism. It is a beautifully acted out portrayal of the process by which God dwells the believer in Christ's body of flesh and bones. God may have said, when He instituted Water Baptism, Let Us have one baptism pictured by each one who submits to it.

All the elements and actors are present each time a true, New Testament, water baptism is administered:

> First - The watery grave is a token of the tomb.
> Second - The Church Body represents His One Body
> of flesh and bones.
> Third - The minister images the Holy Spirit.
> Fourth - The candidate portrays the Lord Jesus Christ
> being crucified, buried and resurrected.

Now For The Pictorial Illustration
The candidate surrenders to the strength of the minister who plunges him into the watery grave. A moment later, he resurrects from the grave of water. All this is what the audience sees. But, the invisible host of the spirit realm sees more, much more. They see Jesus submit to the power of the Father as He is plunged into the grave. The spirits behold the crucified Christ indwelt by many. Again, they see

the Church Body. They see pictured another soul-spirit added to the glorified body of Christ.

Again, they perceive one more Christian added to that local church body. As the angels continue their inspection, they behold the local church-body, a picture to that community, of Christ's one body. Even as the church-body is one body, yet many members, so Christ's glorified body, is one body. Yet! By a miracle of miracles, all believers are in Him, and He is in all believers.

This token, a thing of beauty, is meant to express a deep, deep, truth. A pattern designed to explain or show forth. A picture of God! Dear God, please forgive us, if we, in the world, have marred the picture!

The Seven Ones of God

1 – One Body - Christ's flesh and bone.
2 – One Spirit - God, the Spirit.
3 – One Hope - Christ's.
4 – One Lord - God, The Son.
5 – One Faith - Christ's.
6 – One Baptism - Christ's Calvary.
7 – One Father - God the Father.

The Seven Firsts

Since God elevates these Seven Ones to a superior position, over and above everyone and everything else, we must never lower them to a position or status less than the greatest, hence - "one."

As an illustration: one body could never refer to the Church. Give honor, prestige, yes importance to the Church Body, but never elevate her above her Lord. This is Christ's Glorified Flesh and Bone Body, Christ Himself. Amen!

One is God's Number; Not Man's

Here are the seven ones which have divided and subdivided Christendom into its many different denominations, sects, organized bodies, and ecclesiastical societies. In almost every case, each of these professes to be the True Church, the only right one, the one and only. To back up their contentions, they offer an abundant array of evidence, arguments, outside the Bible proof (?), denominational history, books, and official documents.

There they are on display with their window dressing arrangement of their doctrines, religious forms, practices, ceremonies, and rites. Thus they hope to attract the church shopper by their easy to join, and easy going program,

Hard to Find as The Missing Link

To attempt to discover the Scriptural Church by the above procedure would be as hard to find as the "missing link." Should the world cease talking about a denomination as a church, and begin talking about the New Testament church, it will be discussing a local church.

A physician once inquired, "Oh! There are so many contradictory and conflicting religious voices clamoring for my attention that I almost despair of discovering the truth. Sir, is there no definite and positive method of learning and knowing the truth - the real truth? The answer given this one of the medical profession was the Master's own statement, "Search the Scriptures."

Robbed of Heaven Forever

Since so many ecclesiastical groups may offer very convincing proof that theirs is the one and only church, how may one determine the real truth?

This eternal question is of no small import. A child's eternal welfare, as well as Dad's and Mother's, may depend upon the correct and proper answer. The popularized motto: "join the church of your choice," instead of the church of His choice, in many instances might result in that soul being robbed of heaven forever. Not that locating and joining a right church would save that soul, but, finding the church that preaches the gospel may result in that precious soul finding Christ.

Money Robbers and Soul Robbers

Who is the more vicious criminal, the money robber, or the soul robber? Certainly, Jesus taught that by a soul embracing that which is false may result in that one becoming "Twofold more the child of the devil." What, then, is the church of His choice? Is it not the New Testament church? That is, the one revealed in the Bible? As you search the Scriptures you will find many local churches. Each one preaching the Gospel and picturing Christ to that community.

Since the Bible's one body refers to Christ's own flesh and bone body, Christ Himself, where will you search and find a one denominational Body? One place only. Beloved, one place only! That place - The world!

In fact, in the world, you will find many denominational bodies, and many of them claiming to be the one body of Christ. Blasphemy!

Churches; not Church

"Unto the churches of Galatia." Notice! (Churches plural) (Galatians 1:2). There are the "Seven Churches" of Revelation, chapters two and three. One could duplicate this evidence many more times.

There is but one body, yet, each local church body a picture to that community of that one-body. There is but one Bible, but, many copies. There is but one Lamb of God, yet, many little lambs of the Old Testament - each a type or picture of God's one Lamb.

It would be most incorrect to refer to these churches as the bodies of Christ. Could one correctly say, "The Bibles of God, or the Lambs of God?" Some Bible references do refer to the church in the abstract, but, as an institution only.

The Mystery of the Church

The Greeks had a word called, "ekklesia," from "ek" (out of), and "klesis" (a calling). They used it to designate a "mob" a "gathering of citizens"- or an "assembly of towns-people," our word is "church" or called out ones. This is another instance where God borrowed a word, converted it, made it over, and made it mean what He desired it to mean. Our Lord-God can take a sinner, convert him, change him, indwell him, and make him to be what God desires him to be. He certainly can do the same with a word!

There is but one Book in the Universe which can tell man the true meaning of this converted-word, church; and that Book is the Holy Bible! The meaning of this mysterious word can only be deduced by inquiring into its usage: as employed of God. When our great God selected the word, church, it meant "Called out ones-assembled." Now! Pray tell! Where and when could all these "Called out ones" ever be "assembled?" Praise the Lord! Not on the earth! The first time and place! In the Heavenlies - at the Rapture!

Each Member of a Local Church Body is a Crucified Member of Christ's Body
The Holy Spirit informs us, "This is a great mystery: But I speak concerning the church." First - He informs that we are members of His body (lest any imagine this is the church Body, He immediately informs us He is speaking), of His flesh, and of His bones (Ephesians 5:30).

Our Savior allows a man and his wife to become a type or picture of Jesus and His Bride, the Church. But! Please remember, there is no bride till there is a wedding. This wedding takes place in the sky. Some of the members of that bride in prospect are in Heaven, some are still on the earth; perhaps, some have not as yet been born. After the wedding we will all be one bride!

"That in the dispensation of the fullness of times He might gather together in one all things in Christ, both which are in Heaven, and which are on earth; even in Him (Ephesians 1:10).

Eve; Adam's Bride
Eve being taken from Adam's body has thus been created "bone of his bone and flesh of his flesh" (Genesis 2:23). Although this was the

first surgical operation performed in the world, and a great miracle it was; however, this but pictures the greater miracle of Jesus and the converted sinner becoming one flesh. Christ is in each one, while each and every one is in Him.

His miraculous and omnipresentized flesh and bones body, glorified in the tomb, is now capable of being clothed upon each and every believer. Thus each and every believer is actually a member of His mysterious Flesh and Bones Body.

Our gracious and loving Father, wishing to picture this marvelous truth to each community, assembles a group of crucified called out ones to portray, image, and picture this unparalleled mysterious miracle to that particular area.

The Human Body Serves as an Example of Christ's One Body
God employs the human body to serve as an example of His Son's miraculous body: "For as the body (human body - any) is one, and hath many members (are not all members, hands, feet, eyes, ears, etc., actually a very part of that human body?), and all the members of that one body, being many are one body; So also is Christ" (1 Corinthians 12:12).

But How Could All Believers Be in Christ?
How could all believers be in One Person? By a miracle only! The only-once-performed-miracle is exposed in the following luminous exposition of this verse: "For by One Spirit are we all (Christians) baptized (Notice, please, who the Baptizer is) into One Body."

This one transcending miracle of redemption, the one mighty act of God, planned before the "world's foundation," nothing paralleling it before or since, is the acme of all the creative acts of an Almighty God. That great miracle is baptism!

"One baptism" as meaning the act whereby the One Spirit crucifies, buries, and resurrects each and every individual blood bought believer with Christ. This is in exact accordance with Jesus' own prophetic decree, "Ye shall be baptized with the baptism I am baptized with." By the One Spirit we are all baptized with the same baptism Jesus was baptized with. And each one is baptized together with Him.

One Body Negates All Others

Since there is but one body, one preeminently superior glorified Body, how could this possibly refer to any kind of a church body without negating His? Does not the one render void the other? If this is Jesus' own flesh and bones, then the other is rendered non-existent!

This most superior miracle - mystery "Hath been hid from ages and generations, out now is made manifest to His saints" (Colossians 1:26). By publishing abroad and proclaiming that One Body to be a Church Body, large, small, or universal, is to conceal and withdraw from sight, the peerless, and matchless miracle of Christ being "All and in all."

But! How can our God be "All and in all?" This matchless miracle of His being all and in all is accomplished only by dwelling each individual believer In Himself and abiding in each and every individual believer. This can only be accomplished by our great God, who is omnipresent in His body.

An Invisible and Mystical Universal Body?

Are we to believe in an invisible, mystical, and universal body? Indeed, yes. For, does not our Lord clothe us in the presence of His own mysterious, invisible, flesh and bones body? In order to abide each believer, both in Heaven and one Earth, in His mystical flesh and bones body, would He not have to be trans-universal and omnipresent?

What Church Would the Apostles Join?

If Peter, James, and John were to come down from Heaven, looking for a church to join, with heavenly instructions to "join the church of His choice," what church would they seek? Would it not be a local church? Is there any other revealed in the Bible?

Would not these three Christ Loving Apostles, seek the Local Church that preaches the Gospel and that from the Bible only? As a member of that Local Body, would they not go forth proclaiming the Father's loving kindness as revealed in His redemption plan?

Would not the Apostle Paul admonish all the Christians, with Peter and John affirming "Put ye on the New Man, which is renewed in knowledge after the image of Him that created him: where there is neither Greek nor Jew, circumcision nor uncircumcision, Barbarian, Scythian, bond nor free, but Christ is all and in all" (See Colossians 3:11).

God created man in His own image. But! Man fell. Man lost that image. Again! God created man. In this recreation, God restored that image by creating Christ in you! Is this not the hope of glory!

Study, Discussion & Application Points for Chapter 6

1. Read and Study this chapter.
2. The key verse for this chapter is Galatians 3:26-27: *"For ye are all the children of God by faith in Christ Jesus. For as many of you as have been baptized into Christ have put on Christ."*
3. Dr. Lambert points out the term "one baptism" from Ephesians 4:5. He clearly points out this reference concerns the "Calvary baptism" of our Lord. The water baptism of Jesus points toward the immersion of Christ into the tomb and His subsequent resurrection. Our water baptisms are a clear picture of the work of Jesus and a public statement that we have trusted in Christ for the eradication of our sins. Note the words of Jesus in Matthew 20:22-23 and consider that Jesus is talking about future events (His water baptism had clearly already happened). Read and study Romans 6:1-5 and ask the Holy Spirit for instruction as you write down your thoughts.
4. Continue in Romans 6 and note these key words and verses:
   • Know (knowing) in v. 3, 6 & 9. What does God want us to know?

- Reckon (meaning "apply") in v. 11. What knowledge does God want us to apply? How is this done? What will be the results?
- Yield in v. 13. What are we to yield? Who are we to yield to? What will be the results?

5. Consider how this chapter fits into the theology of Galatians 2:20: I am crucified with Christ: nevertheless I live; yet not I, but Christ liveth in me: and the life which I now live in the flesh I live by the faith of the Son of God, who loved me, and gave himself for me.

7

THE MYSTERY OF ONE FAITH

One Faith

Is this "one faith" a denomination? Is this "one faith" some system of religious beliefs? Is this "one faith," man's faith? Is this "one faith," God's, or man's? This is neither a denominational system of religious beliefs, nor man's personal faith in God. But! " the faith of the Son of God!" This is the "one faith" of the Son! This is perfect faith; Satan beating faith!

From whom does man receive faith? Allow the Lord to answer from Holy Writ. "In whom we have boldness and access with confidence by the faith of Him" (Ephesians 3:12).

Not Your Faith but Christ's

Even as Christ dwells His righteousness within the believer, so He dwells His perfect faith. This is not Christ's faith, in a person. But! Christ's faith, in person. In precisely the same manner as He dwells the Spirit of Eternal Life within your body, just so, He dwells the Spirit of faith. "We having the same Spirit of faith..." (2 Corinthians 4:13).

We Are Saved by Grace Through Faith

"For by grace are ye saved through faith, and that not of yourselves: it is the gift of God" (Eph. 2:8-9). However! It is not your faith, through which God saves and keeps you. God does not look unto your wavering faith as the basis for your salvation. Your poor faith is too imperfect. Your merciful and loving Father considers your precious soul of greater value than to trust it with your little faith. He must find a perfect faith. Where else would God find a perfect faith, but, in His Son?

Sealed Secrets

Hence, "one faith." One perfect faith - none other like His. Even in this He must have the preeminence. This is not merely a divinely implanted principle. This is Christ's "one faith" manifested through the believer. The secret of "His faith," is the secret of His presence. Magnificent mystery! "Christ in you, the hope of glory."

Startling Mystery

May we consider the startling truth of the Christian's death by crucifixion? Astonishing, if true! "Always bearing about in the body the dying of the Lord Jesus, that the life also of Jesus might be made manifest in our mortal flesh" (2 Corinthians 4:10).

Notice: "Bearing about in the body the dying of the Lord Jesus." You may rightfully inquire, if my body is dead, as taught here and elsewhere, by what power do I still live?

Before we answer the above titanic question, we first should assemble several passages that teach the Christian's actual bodily death at the time of conversion. Notice the Bible's own terminology:

1. "And if Christ be in you, the body is dead because of sin" (Romans 8:10).
2. "For ye are dead and your life is hid with Christ in God" (Colossians 3:3).
3. "I am crucified with Christ" (Galatians 2:20).
4. "Wherefore, my brethren, ye also are become dead to the law by the body of Christ" (Romans 7:4).

Why Are We Dead?

5. "For he that is dead is freed from sin" (Romans 6:7).
6. "That as sin hath reigned unto death, even so might grace reign through" (Romans 5:21).
7. "How shall we that are dead to sin, live any longer therein?" (Romans 6:2).
8. "Knowing this, that our old man is crucified with Him, that the body of sin might be destroyed, that henceforth we should not serve sin" (Romans 6:6).
9. "But yield yourselves unto God, as those that are alive from the dead" (Romans 6:13).

I guess the only workable method that will keep a man from sinning, is to put him to death. Sin can reign only unto death; according to the Holy Spirit in Romans 5:21. Can a dead man sin? God's answer: "He that is dead is freed from sin". Would a police officer arrest a dead man?

Now for A Titanic question and For An Answer a Spiritual Rocket-Burst
Does not your soul ask this question? If my body is dead, how do I happen to still have life? Certainly the Bible teaches over and over, my body is dead; but, by what means or force do I still move?

Better check your controls, Christian, lest you enter into a spiritual "power dive," after you learn the answer. For the answer is, the mover dwells within! As you were crucified with Him, He fashioned Himself into your being; transmitting His miraculous life-power through your flesh.

Paul's Astonishing Explanation
The Apostle marveled at his own new life. When he Cried, "I am crucified with Christ..." Paul, does not crucifixion kill? How can you be crucified and yet live?

He exuberantly answers, "I live, yet not I, but Christ liveth in me (Christ liveth!): and the life which I now live in the flesh I live by the faith (There is another key word we have been looking for… Faith! With! His one faith!) of the Son of God, who loved me, and gave Himself for me" (Galatians 2:20).

Super Miracle of Miracles
A new Principle of Life: Spiritual Life Acting Upon the Flesh
Friend of mine! You are a new creation! Calculate the eternal value of this! His resurrected, eternal body-power, flows through your flesh. He actuates by His transforming power. He, the Mover, moves you. His eternal spiritual life, manifested through your flesh. By "the faith and operation of God" He actuates, energizes, impels, and operates the New Creature (See Colossians 2:11-13). "Stand fast in the power of His might!" "Put off … the old man…" "… Put on the New Man…" (See Ephesians 4:22-24).

A List of Verses Proving This New Life is Christ ~ Christ's Heart Beats Within Your Own

1. "For ye are dead, and your life is hid with Christ in God. When Christ who is your life (notice: He is your life), shall appear, then shall ye appear with Him in glory" (Colossians 3:3-4).
2. "Quickened (made alive) together with Him" (Colossians 2:13).
3. "And if Christ be in you, the body is dead because of sin; but the Spirit is life (Spirit is life) because of righteousness" (Romans 8:10).
4. "… The life also of Jesus (notice carefully: The life of Jesus) might be manifest in our mortal (human) flesh" (2 Corinthians 4:11).

5. "... That the life of Jesus (Jesus own life) might be made manifest in our body " (Notice: Jesus' life manifested in our mortal body) (2 Corinthians 4:10). He keeps you alive every minute, and moment by moment!

6. "...Yield yourselves unto God, as those that are alive from the dead ..." (Romans 6:13).

7. "Now if we be dead with Christ, we believe that we shall also live with Him" (Romans 6:8).

Love Magnified

It was not at all difficult for our great Savior God to discover a means whereby He could keep alive each one who is crucified with Him. Out of tender love and universal knowledge, He created Himself-within each blood bought believer. Each Christ-in-one! His tender, loving, heart beats within ours!

His Faith, Not Yours, Keeps You Alive and Sustains You

Regard this marvelous truth! It is His faith, not the exercise of your faith that keeps you alive. Rest easy! Be assured! Your body is now His temple. You are immortal until He is done with your body of flesh. His faith is continually being exercised as He so patiently abides His loving presence within.

Not Having Mine Own Righteousness

The Apostle Paul did not expect to enter Heaven upon the basis of his own righteousness or his own faith. "And be found in Him, not having mine own righteousness, which is of the law, but that which is through the faith of Christ (saved by grace through the faith of Christ), the righteousness which is of God by faith" (Philippians 3:9).

Justified By Christ's Faith

Again the Apostle Paul declares, Justification is by the faith of Jesus Christ. He affirms he has been crucified with Christ; yet still lives.

"Yet not I" But, the indwelling Christ lives for both of them. And this, by the faith of the son of God. This is Christ's faith in God's faithful operation, which keeps alive the one who has been crucified with Christ (1 Corinthians 2:5).

One Faith

"For by grace are ye saved, through faith and that not of yourselves," God does not look unto you and your wavering faith for the basis of your salvation. Your poor faith is so imperfect. Your merciful Father considers your precious soul of greater value than to trust it with your little faith. He must find a perfect faith. But, where, among men, will He find that faith? Where else but in His Son?

Thus, that "One Faith" is His faith. One perfect faith - none other like His. Even in this He must have the preeminence. Just as He dwells His perfect righteousness within the believer, so, also, He dwells His perfect faith.

Our Two Irish Friends Pat and Mike

Pat and Mike were on their way to work, one morning, when Pat suggested the two of them cut across a vacant lot, "Its closer, be golly," he explained. Suddenly, however, Mike saw cause for alarm, "Look out, Pat," he cried excitedly, as he pointed toward the ground, "there's a snake, as long as yore bloomi'n arm." "Schore, and let's keel 'em," retorted Pat, "We'el bash his blarsted head in."

By this time a couple, Irishmen were very intent upon locating instruments of assassination. One found a club of enormous proportions, (for bashing purposes) while the other located a stone, about half as large as a tub. With these instruments of execution, our two Irish heroes made short work of the "slithering varmint;" as the elongated one came to a sudden and untimely end. No doubt about it; they killed a snake! After a hard day's work, the two pals decided to take the same short-cut on their way home.

As they came upon the scene of the morning's reptilian execution episode, they both stared wide eyed at what they saw. The snake, just then, slowly but certainly, wiggled the utmost point of its "infernal" body. This was just too much, this undue departure from the ordinary. "By-jabbers, Pat," exclaimed the agitated, unbelieving Mike, "I tho't we keeled'em." The flabbergasted, but quick retorting Pat came up with a bit of expert elucidation, "Oh! He's dead all right; we keeled 'em, but he ain't found it ouht yet."

May we suggest that many Christians, though dead to sin, haven't found it out yet. The slithering serpent, Satan, has blinded their eyes.

The Mystery of One Hope
Here is another of the "Seven Ones of God." The seven "firsts." Seven "no others." Only "one" of each. Now, we come to "One Hope." One Hope, for Heaven and Earth. We shall make the extremely startling discovery that the "One Hope" is the Lord. "Blessed is the man that trusteth in the Lord, and who's Hope the Lord is." (Jeremiah 17:7).

Looking for that Blessed Hope and the Glorious Appearing of the Great God and Our Savior, Jesus Christ
Can we not rightly say, "He, the Lord, is our Blessed Hope?" "Christ in you, The Hope of glory." "We are heirs according to the hope of eternal life having been justified by His grace" (Titus 3:7). The Holy Ghost, the Author of hope, creates within you a bountiful supply of hope, drawing on his never diminishing reservoir. "For we through the Spirit wait for the hope of righteousness by faith" (Galatians 5:5). Christ is the One Hope of Israel Acts 28:29). Is He not the only hope of the "Sputnik-Frightened" world?

Mighty Works Can Only be Accomplished Through Mighty Faith; Almighty Works Can Only be Accomplished Through Almighty Faith
Heaven depends upon the faith of God's children in order to accomplish mighty works. "And He did not many mighty works there because of their unbelief" (Matthew 13:58).

However! In the bigger matters of paramount importance, such as salvation, resurrection of the dead in Christ, Rapture of the Saints, the defeat of Satan's Hosts, and the bringing to pass all God's recorded prophecies; ordinary man's faith will not suffice. Therefore, God must find a perfect overcoming and Satan mastering faith.

Where would God find the necessary Almighty Faith? God's holy spotless Son can be depended upon to manifest a perfect faith; a faith in God to overcome all obstacles of the arch enemy, Satan. Hence, "One Faith." The Man, Christ Jesus, being the only One with a perfect faith, is the only One in whom both Heaven and Earth can hope. God must also have an object of faith; One in whom both Heaven and Earth can hope; hence, He, Jesus the Christ is the One Hope.

Study, Discussion & Application Points for Chapter 7

1. Read and Study this chapter. Note that Ephesians 4:4-6 speaks of the One Faith and the One Hope.

2. The key verse for this chapter is Philippians 3:9: *And be found in him, not having mine own righteousness, which is of the law, but that which is through the faith of Christ, the righteousness which is of God by faith:*

3. We are saved by the mercy and grace of God. And it is the mercy and grace of God that keeps us saved. Some have struggled with their own faith, knowing it is imperfect. Doubts continue to swirl through their head as Satan continues to fire his evil darts. Read Matthew 28:16-17 and note the issue of doubting has been with Christians from the beginning. Consider the "One Faith" mentioned in Ephesians 4 and know that it is the faith of Jesus Christ, who dwells within us that is sufficient. With this in mind, look up the following verses and ask God to reveal His thoughts to you:
   - Galatians 2:20
   - 2 Corinthians 4:7-11

- Romans 6:8
- Ephesians 4:22-24

4. Dr. Lambert shows clearly the Bible teaches we are new crea-
    tures at the moment of our salvation. Jesus, "the Mover, moves
    us. His eternal spiritual life is now manifested through our
    flesh. He actuates, energizes, impels and operates the new
    creature." Read Colossians 2:11-13 several times and jot down
    your thoughts as God reveals them to you.

5. This chapter points out that Jesus is our "Blessed Hope". It
    is Jesus that has the perfect life and perfect faith. It is Jesus
    that will accomplish the eternal events in our lives. It is Jesus,
    living inside us, that gives us the power to overcome the flesh-
    ly strongholds in our lives. Read the following passages and
    write down your thoughts:
    - Ephesians 2:3-6
    - Ephesians 3:19-20

8

THE MYSTERY OF INIQUITY AS IT PERTAINS TO THE UNSAVED

"For the mystery of iniquity doth already work" (See 2 Thessalonians 2:7). Mystery! Iniquity! Works! Notice: "The mystery of iniquity... works". Iniquity works! Great activity! But, where? In behind the scenes! Back in the darkness of the Unseen World, slithering - foaming - imps of Hell!

What is This Terrible Mystery?

What is this terrorizing mystery? The alarming mystery is in the vicious, mystifying method of procedure, Satan and his host operates upon the minds of men. Whosoever controls the mind of a man can direct that one's life. As horrible as this may be, this is the manner in which the - Arch Foe manipulates his subjects.

Beelzebub heads a vast company of the most vicious and wicked creatures in the Universe. Having renounced their allegiance to God, they now follow their leader, whose main business is to people the Caverns of Hell with the souls of men.

Operation Damnation

The mystery of the devil's hellish activities upon the thinking processes of the unsaved is revealed in the Word of God; which condemns these foul Spirits. "But if our Gospel be hid, it is hid to them that are lost" (2 Corinthians 4:3-4). But now could a thing as well known as the Crucifixion be concealed? The fact of it is not withdrawn from sight; but its purpose is hidden.

Although the lost sinner has already been punished in the Person of his Substitute; even pardoned, and the gift of salvation tendered, yet the most difficult problem of the soul-winner is to get this glorious truth across to him. As the winner of souls approaches the lost subject to inform concerning the Good News, an evil spirit agitates the mind of the one to be won, and most often registers great displeasure. The imaginative processes, of the deceived one, are thus stirred as he feels an inward urge to resist; imagining he is being unduly pressed, and even imposed upon.

Let us Alone
"And there was in their synagogue a man with an unclean spirit; and he cried out, saying, Let us alone" (Mark 1:23-24). The ghastly truth was, that man was not doing the talking. His vocal cords and speaking apparatus were possessed of this devil. Often times a lost sinner, on the point of being won to Christ, will cry out, "Leave us alone"; and this often times with an oath.

There is a Dead Line For the Soul and Satan Knows It
The demons know full well there is a point of no return. A dead-line for the soul! We may term it; Destruction Point. The Black Curtain Task Force makes every effort to hinder and oppress; and burden and harass till that line is reached. They will cause the poor lost soul to postpone, and putting off acceptance of Christ's offer for salvation, intending to thus trap their victim.

Desecration of God's Name by Oaths
Another contrivance of man's enemy is to blaspheme through lips that should be praying. Cursing is without temptation, except as it is inspired of fallen angels. Soon the deceived is so in the habit of

profaning the Holy One's name that it is difficult for him to conceive how God could be used in any other way. Each time he exercises himself in this sacrilegious manner he is stepping that much nearer that dead-line. God forbid!

Satan Blinds Minds

"In whom the god (devil) of this world hath blinded the minds of them that believe not, lest the light of the glorious Gospel of Christ who is the image of God, should shine unto them" (2 Corinthians 4:4).

Where is This Evil One?

The unsaved sinner man may be indwelt by one or more spirits of evil, "... according to the prince of the power of the air, the spirit that now worketh (there is that word: worketh) in the children of disobedience" (Ephesians 2:2). The above verse is only one of many that teach an unsaved person may be indwelt by an fallen angel.

Satan Broadcasts Evil Imaginations Upon Minds

False imaginations concerning our Savior-God are often beamed to register upon the mind of the Christ rejecter. "But I fear lest by any means, as the serpent beguiled Eve through his subtlety, so your minds should be corrupted from the simplicity that is in Christ" (2 Corinthians 11:1-3).

"For the weapons of our warfare are not carnal, but mighty through God to the pulling down of strongholds; casting down imaginations, and every high thing that exalteth itself against the knowledge of God, and bringing into captivity every thought to the obedience of Christ" (2 Corinthians 10:4-5).

According to the above verses, Satan operates through the mind of the unsuspecting lost soul. Eve listened to words. Eve's Children listen to thoughts. "O foolish Galatians, who hath bewitched you, that ye should not obey the truth" (Galatians 3:1).

Isaiah exhorted the sinner to "forsake thy thoughts" (Isaiah 55:7). The man who harkens to his own thoughts is doomed! Take heed!

Observe a sly little secret! Satan tempts by remote control. The human mind is his area of operation.

Some Embrace Doctrines of Devils

"If any man (or an angel from Heaven) preaches any other Gospel ... let him be accursed" (Galatians 1:8-9). If the god of this world can regulate the devil-indwelt man's thoughts by inducing him to embrace doctrines of devils he has the man doomed above ground. "Now the Spirit speaketh expressly, that in the latter times some shall depart from the faith, giving heed to seducing spirits, and doctrines of devils" (1 Timothy 4:1). Hunches won't do!

Seducing Spirits Induce the Possessed One to Take Away From the Bible

"And if any man shall take away from the words of the Book of this prophecy, God shall take away his part out of the Book of Life, and out of the Holy City" (Revelation 22:19). There goes the loss of some one's mansion!

How is this done? How may one take away from the word of God? Is it not by disbelieving the plain Word of God? Is it not disbelieving the doctrine of Hell? Is it not disbelieving the Virgin Birth? Is it not submitting one's mind and heart to the truth of the Atonement? Is it by making light of the Sacred Scriptures? Is it by questioning the Bible being the product Of God? "To execute judgment upon all, and to convince all that are ungodly among them of all their ungodly deeds which they have ungodly committed, and all their hard speeches which ungodly sinners have spoken against Him" (Jude 15).

The Trust is to be Loved

"And with all deceivableness of unrighteousness in them that perish; because they received not the love of the Truth that they might be saved. That they all might be damned who believed not the truth, but had pleasure in unrighteousness" (2 Thessalonians 2:10).

Satan is the Prosecuting Attorney

In the Day of Judgment, Satan, who knows the Word and the Law, will prosecute the sinner to the fullest extent of that Law, by demanding the second death penalty. In spite of all that a loving Savior could do, in spite of all that loving friends and family could do, Satan will proclaim, and I won. I demand this one, who violated God's law, be sent to the eternal Lake of Fire!

To know and understand that Satan can bewitch, by beaming his Christ-rejecting thoughts upon the lost man's mind; to Know and understand Satan is doing this in order that he might thus condemn at the Judgment, and yet, continue to resist the Gospel plea, is to commit one's self to self-inflicted eternal torment. May our sinner friends, turn from self to God, and trust His marvelous enduring love.

When Satan demands the death penalty; unless one has secured the services of Attorney Jesus, and thus received His pardon, these awful words will ring through that soul forever: Depart from Me ye worker of iniquity! The guilty one will doubtless, in anguish, cry, "O, God! How awful, I was pardoned from this infernal place, but! I was deceived into rejecting my blood bought pardon".

City of Ghosts

This Unknown lost soul will through the endless ages attempt again and again to commit suicide; But, Alas! In that World of Lost Ones they do not die!

9

THE MYSTERY OF INIQUITY AS IT PERTAINS TO THE SAVED; FOR WE WRESTLE

"For we wrestle not against flesh and blood, but against principalities, against powers, against the rulers of the darkness of this world" (Ephesians 6:12).

The Christian grapples not with flesh and blood beings as with humans, but a dark Company of centuries trained fiends. This perverted host works the mystery of iniquity upon the human race "With all deceivableness of unrighteousness in them that perish, by a horrible and uncanny process. The consideration of what is to follow will present so hideous a picture as to strike terror into one's soul.

Right there - by you, but back out of sight, is an eerie being, who is your exact image! An ageless being who is capable of fashioning himself into a reptile, hog, or human being. How does he accomplish this? By personalizing himself within the one he wishes to dominate. This one we wrestle!

The Christian Once Indwelt by This Evil Spirit

Is it not shocking to contemplate what might have happened in the days before your salvation? Were you not inspirited by this evil one? "The spirit that now worketh in the children of disobedience"

(Ephesians 2:2). "When the unclean spirit is gone out of a man ..." (Luke 11:24).

Who are the "Rulers of the Darkness of this world"? Who are the "Principalities and Powers"?

Is not a principality a territory or jurisdiction of a Prince? Super-abundant Beings, who exercise rule called Principalities and Powers, operate over cities, states, and nations. These hateful creatures are well organized, centuries trained, and of supernatural power and intelligence. Daniel was with-stood by the Prince of Persia, a powerful fallen angel.

Satan Entered The Body of the King of Tyrus

Satan personalized himself in the body of King Tyrus. This horrendous host of antagonists employ themselves upon the minds of kings and rulers as well as the man in the street. When Satan personalized himself in the body of King Tyrus, God declared him, "Full of wisdom, perfect in beauty, and thou sealest up the sum" (Ezekiel 28:12).

Duped of the Devils; Then a deceiver of people

Now we can better understand the actions of Hitler and Pharaoh the Hell Hound; Stalin, and the present day dictators of godless Russia. The prince of demons, the ruler of the darkness of this world, today pits one national ruler against another. The modern Satan-called minister is actually duped of the devil. Thus he becomes a dupe-devil. Satan is the most powerful being off the Throne of God. Satan aspires to be "like the Most High". The leading Devil is now, according to the Apostle Paul, "The god of this world" (2 Corinthians 4:4).

The Mystery of the False Ministers of our Present World

"Be loved, believe not every spirit ... Because many false prophets are gone out into the world" (1 John 4:1). The devil doctrines being promulgated today are the result of the diabolic system whereby demons form themselves into human's bodies and thus become Satan called ministers who appear as angels of light.

Diablo Sauce
Speaking of False Ministers, Satan's missionaries are being sent to the Regions Below. "The mystery of iniquity doth already work." These may be blind leaders of the blind, but they are practicing diabolism (commerce with the devil).

Fallen Angels; Fallen Men
These fallen angels, who are now ruling over Principalities and Powers, cities, states, and nations, resent God's Children, because we will one day (a thousand year day) hold their then vacated offices. We will rule and reign with the Lord, over these same cities, territories and nations. Read Luke 19:17-19.

The Goon Squad
These by-products of Satan are often offered flattering positions of wealth and ecclesiastical power, to help promote the "deformed and misshapen Gospel of Hell". What is the Gospel of Hell? What is this supposed Good News? What is this Glad Tidings concerning the Pit? What is this that Satan is anxious to have published by his infernal demons-controlled False Angels of Light? Is it not the devil doctrine of No Hell? These Word-Wresters, dupes of the devils, twist the Scriptures to their own damnation. This reminds me of the fellow who committed suicide. His suicide note read, "I stabbed myself to death to see what it felt like."

Self-Inflicted Torment
One of the tricks of the devil, this Old Wrestler, is to trip. Now, these who are thus bedeviled, as a reward, must suffer a trip to the Violently-mad Ward of the Asylum of the Universe. There it is night forever!

Angels Were Earth Dwellers Long Before Adam. Exhuming Their Dead Past

From out of the darkness of the Unseen World, came these denizens of the past. These were earth dwellers long before the presentation of Adam's race of human beings. Angels, perhaps, were merely spoken into existence, like the beautiful pristine world they were to inhabit until their fall. But not so man. He must be "hand formed," God in-breathed, and fashioned in God's image.

The power of Satan's displeasure must now be brought to bear. Had not God said to this first human pair, "replenish the earth?" God's entire purpose for man on the earth, in fact the answer to the age old question of "Why am I here", is packaged in this one-word command, "replenish!" God is taking out a new order of sons. For each fallen angel, a soul must be born.

Man Fell Hence the New Birth

As quickly as the cry rang out through the City of Light, "Adam is fallen! Adam is fallen!;" God issued a new proclamation to man, "ye must be born again."

Satan Operates the World System as the God of This World

This Angels of Hell Tribe, unseen, operates their Black Curtain, be-hind the scenes, master minding the World System, by mastering the minds of men. As surely as God has set up the Gospel Preaching Church System, to send men to Heaven, just as certainly, Satan has set up the World System to send men to Hell.

This is how his Satanic Majesty works: Satan hates God, and wish-es to profane Him. Thus his hellish personality is fused with man's, by way of his demons. This results in the shockingly, ugly, overwhelm-ing control of that individual being. Thus, this one controlled by the

"Phantoms of the Under World, dislikes God, hates the Bible, avoids Church, resents and resists all Gospel appeals.

A Lover of the World is an Enemy of God's
"Know ye not that the friendship of the world is enmity with God. Whosoever therefore will be a friend of the world is the enemy of God" (James 4:4). Satan introduced sin into the world in order to insult God. He brought the World System into existence in order that man might practice sin.

In full sight of God, day after day, God's enemies indulge in sin, curse His name, and blaspheme His proffered gift of salvation. How could poor mortal unsaved man, who actually wishes to spend eternity in Heaven, to the same degree as others, continue to resist God and thus doom and damn his own soul?

Men do not, of themselves, wish to do this. Man has no desire to spend eternity in the penitentiary of the universe. Then why does he expose his own soul to the blazing torments of Hell? The answer is found by a consideration of the following incident.

When the lost man in Mark 1:24, cried out, "Let us alone;" the hideous truth is, that flesh and bone and blood man was not the real spokesman. This was not his own action. His mind is deranged, he is bewitched of Satan. Read Galatians 3:1.

Blackness of the Pit Darkens the Mind
The evil spirits humanize themselves by inspiriting flesh. The demonized mind registers the personality of the Dark One. The mind is blinded to the "aimed light of the Truth," by the Devil's thoughts of Christ rejection, and excuse making. Like a window shade over the mind, Satan shuts out the Light.

This Master Criminal demonizes the mind of the educated as well as uneducated by inspiriting himself and gradually taking control, in extreme cases the Master of Minds fuses his own murderous intent into the thinking processes of his victim, while the mind goes

MYSTERY OF THE AGES

berserk. The frenzied mind often destroys those whom he loves best; then turns to destroy self.

The writer recently knew of a man who announced he would blow his brains out with his shotgun; then used his family as his audience. Consider this carefully, Christian, winner of souls; until released and delivered, our lost friend may be trapped in a body with a demon.

The demonized one is not always a bad fellow, or a great crook; in fact, often times he is a very moral gentleman. More often the evil spirit will allow his victim to be self-righteous; feeling no need of God. The snaky killers must not allow themselves to become known to the one they indwell; just keeping him from the Lord is their main task.

Christians as Objects of Demonic Wiles
Christian, this is the Invisible Host of Hell whom we "wrestle." As frightening as it may seem, the weird truth is we, too, are objects of demon wiles. The singular difference being, they cannot indwell bodies which have become the temples of the Lord.

Satan Broadcasts His Hellish Imaginations
Although demon forces cannot indwell the body of a "Christ-in-one" they have fearful methods whereby they broadcast their thoughts onto the mind of the Christian, "We wrestle not against flesh and blood, but against principalities, against powers…"

The Christian, my friend, may be "bewitched of the satanic Host. Bewitching has to do with the mind. Christian, you are not the only one who can think through your own mind. God can, Satan can, and you do. Now, we must remember the Galatians Epistle is addressed to Christians whose minds are being bewitched.

No Longer I that Do It
The Apostle Paul's desire was to live a most victorious life before his Lord. "For to will is present with me; but how to perform that which is

good I find not?" There was an overpowering hindrance, somewhere be-hind the scenes, wasn't there? "For that which I do I allow not: For what I would, that I do not; but what I hate that do I" (See Romans 7:14-25). Paul knew and taught that the Old Man was dead by crucifixion. The Spirit through him wrote, "He that is dead is freed from sin."

Can a dead man sin? "Knowing this, that our old man is crucified with Him, that the body of sin might be destroyed, that henceforth we should not serve sin. For he that is dead is freed from sin". "Being then made free from sin, ye became the servants of righteousness." "We are dead to the law by the body of Christ" (Romans 7:4).

"Likewise reckon yourselves to be dead indeed unto sin, but alive unto God through Jesus Christ our Lord" (Romans 6:11). Certainly, the Scriptures, which cannot lie, say, "He that is dead is freed from sin." The Spirit is not talking about embalmed men, but, a crucified Christian, whose body of sin has thus been destroyed. Sin having no power over that one, can no longer reign over him.

Is there then, an answer to this perplexing mystery? Indeed there is! But, first let us listen as Paul deepens the mystery by stat-ing, "For the good that I would I do not." Like all true Christians, who love their Lord and desire to please Him with a better, much better life, the Apostle cried, "But the evil which I would not, that I do" (Romans 7:19).

What is This Mystery? What is Sin?

Sin may be any act or thought which cannot be defended at the Throne of God. Sin is missing the mark! Sin is anything short of per-fection. "All have sinned and come short of the glory of God." God's glory is His perfection. All men are sinners. As the Irishman con-fessed, "My wife used to say, before I married her, 'I wouldn't marry the best man on earth.' "And she didn't either, folks, she didn't!"

Sin as a Noun

We have been using the word sin as a verb, but, may we now consider it as a noun. Sin as a noun, as used in the Bible, represents a principle or source of action, or as an inward element producing acts of wrong. Again sin is spoken of as an organized power, acting through the members of the body. Sin, in order to work must have an organic instrument.

Sin is often personified in the Bible
In many passages sin is conceived as representing a person. Sin is thus personified in such passages as, "Sin hath reigned unto death" (Romans 5:21). "Sin shall not have dominion over you" (Romans 6:14). Now, we know sin is an abstraction, an idea or principle; not a personal being. However, in behind that abstraction is a "personal Being".

A Personal Being Behind Sin
An "eerie one" who forms the sin idea in the mind, impelling it with the power of desire, stands back in the shadows, out of sight. He is a charmer who can bewitch. This is temptation. This infernal creature understands the secrets of enchantment and sorcery. He can vex and tangle the mind; cast a spell of confusion upon it. By fashioning a mental picture upon the thinking processes, this fiend, creates a craving for some forbidden thing, is this not the manner in which temptation from within is conceived? Pictures and suggestions from without, pictures and the power of suggestion from within, are all used of this Evil Charmer to tempt.

Sin is the Torrid Breath of Satan
The Christian must be on constant guard. "Bringing into captivity ever thought to the obedience of Christ" (2 Corinthians 10:5). "O foolish Galatians. who hath bewitched you" (Galatians 3:1)? Who, not what, hath bewitched you? Thus, Christian, we wrestle. This, a dirty wrestler, lurks in the shadows of the unseen world. He knows rules not at all; he knows all the holds and tricks of the trade. He is a desperate antagonist who wrestles with no holds barred. This is not, however, a hand to hand dual, but a mind to mind death struggle.

No wonder we are admonished of the Spirit to have the "Mind of Christ." His Spirit is within the Christian to catch those thoughts and banish them before they become sin. "And the peace of God, which passeth all understanding, shall keep your hearts and minds through Jesus Christ" (Philippians 4:7).

No Longer I That Do It
"Now it is no more I that do it, but sin that dwelleth in me" (Romans 7:17). Paul discovered that in his flesh dwelleth no good thing (verse 18). Sin in the body is like electricity in a copper wire. It must have a compelling force or power to move it. As volts are power to electricity, so "devils" are to sin.

When Adam sinned, there began to dwell in man's flesh a nature that desires to sin; hence, "a fallen nature." Thus we are, by nature the children of wrath (Ephesians 2:3). For this reason we receive a New Nature by virtue of the new birth. The flesh body is "conceived in sin and shapen in iniquity" (Psalm 51:5).

"Now if I do that I would not, it is no more I that do it, but sin that dwelleth in me" (Romans 7:20). Paul was most willing to obey God perfectly. In fact in his mind he "served the law of God." But he observed that in certain members of his flesh there were cravings and lusts. The Apostle has already told us in Chapter Six, that the old man is dead, and the body of sin destroyed. Paul understands this, believes it, and knows it is true; but, he is still having a "warfare."

Can A Dead Man Sin?
Considering the fact that the Christian's body of sin is dead how is it that he still has sin to confess? He that is dead is freed from sin (Romans 6:7). Sin shall not have dominion over you (Romans 6:14). Yet we still cry out, O God! Forgive us our sins! If we Christians say that we have no sin, we deceive ourselves, and the truth is not in us. Verify this by reading 1 John 1:8. If we confess our sins, He is faithful

and just to forgive us our sins, and to cleanse us from all unrighteousness" (1 John 1:9).

Our problem, then, is since we are dead to sin, by crucifixion, how is it possible for us to sin? Can there possibly be a solution to this mystery? Yes! God's own statement through this same Apostle clears up the mystery. "We wrestle not against flesh and blood" (Eph. 6:12). Harken! "But ye are not in the flesh"

We Have Been Wrestling the Wrong Fellow

Have we been wrestling the wrong fellow? Could one ever win a wrestling match if his opponent were a corpse? Just how would one make him "Holler Uncle?" We have been dragging a stinking dead body around, and trying to get the corruptible thing to cease from being an offense. Paul cried out in despair, "O wretched man that I am! Who shall deliver me from the body of this death?" (Romans 7:24).

Now we know who our real opponent is not! It is not self! Not if self is not in the body of sin. "But ye are not in the flesh." "When we were in the flesh" (Romans 7:5). Has not the body of sin been destroyed? Besides, ye are not in that body. Who then is our opponent? Beloved, we wrestle principalities and powers. These evil ones, who are fallen angels, are our adversaries.

We Have Overcome Them

Our elder brother, the Lord Jesus Christ, saw this big bully and delivered him a good licking; our Father informs us that we have overcome them: because "greater is He that is in you, than he that is in the world" (1 John 4:4).

Not In the Flesh; A Miracle of the New Birth

Picture, please three booklets: One red; One white; One brown. Allow these three to represent the soul, body, and the spirit. Place the white one, representing the soul, within the brown one, which corresponds to the body. There now, you have natural man; a soul within a body. Allow this simple demonstration to make plain two tremendous Bible truths:

1. The Body is dead!
2. Ye are not in the flesh body!

Now, may we demonstrate death by slowly removing the white book (the soul) from within the brown book (the body). The body without the soul is dead. Drop the soul to the floor, allowing this to picture the disembodied soul falling into the Pit. Hand the body-booklet to the man nearest you, in the audience, pretending he is the undertaker. The soul ceases to live longer upon the earth because the earth-body, by virtue of death, is no longer tenantable. The disembodied soul could not enter Heaven without a spirit-body. He cannot enter Heaven without a born-again-spirit.

Calvary's Crucifixion – Death Applied
Now gather up the three booklets, and start all over. Place the soul in the body. This is a lost man, physically alive. But, this man is dead spiritually. Pick up the red booklet, and explain it represents the spirit. You may now show your audience how God puts the new convert to death by applying Calvary. Remove the white-soul booklet from the brown-body. Explain this is the Christian's death. He is no longer in the "flesh."

Place the soul in the spirit. Quote: "But ye are not in the flesh, but in the Spirit." As you place the Spirit-booklet (with the soul safe inside) into the body-booklet, you may ask the Scripture question, "What? Know ye not that your body is the temple of the Holy Ghost which is in you" (1 Corinthians 6:19). This excellent little demonstration quickly puts across the idea of the New Birth, as well as its necessity.

The Body is Dead But the Spirit is Life
By an examination of the three booklets, while in this arrangement, you may show that the soul is actually in the Spirit of Christ, and not in the body. The secret of the Christian's victory is to surrender the body unconditionally to the One who indwells it. He can master the devil, for He is the devil's Master.

Further, you may show that the soul is not in the body; therefore the body is dead. Physical death is the separation of the soul from the body. Is it not? Since the soul is not in the body, the Scriptures can rightly say, "The body is dead." The soul is now in the Spirit of Christ.

The Spirit is Life
Although the body is dead because of sin, the life of this new creature is the Spirit. "The Spirit is life because of righteousness." True, the body is dead because the soul is no longer in it; but, Christ has taken up His abode there to animate it. Is He not able to resurrect it, and keep it alive? Your body is now the temple of the Holy One.

When Christ, Who is Our Life...
Christ's blessed heart must beat within our own. The old man was crucified and destroyed while two (you and Christ) have become one new creature. "If any man be in Christ, He is a new creature." "He who hath the Son, hath life."

You are Passed From Death Unto Life
Christian friend of mine, you shall never die again. You died when you trusted Jesus as your Savior and deliverer. You have now done all the physical dying you are ever going to do. All that is now left to do in order to enter Heaven is to make your exodus and home going. God has now placed you where the wicked one toucheth you not (see 1 John 5:18). "Your life is hid with Christ in God."

Your Body is now Dead to Sin; But Alive to Righteousness
Consider a musical instrument; like it, your body is dead. An artist may produce music through that instrument, while an amateur may damage it. Now your body is an instrument purchased of God, "Ye are not your own"; you are now dead to wrong, set apart of God, to be used of His Son as an instrument of righteousness. Do not allow the Evil One to use your body as an instrument of sin. Unthinkable! God forbid! "How shall we that are dead to sin, live any longer therein?"

Before Salvation, Satan Dwelt Within
Prior to your salvation, a demon dwelt within. It would not allow God to use your body, for it was his property. By means of the cross, Satan and his host were defeated. Satan's power was nullified. His right to hold sinners as slaves for indwellment came to an end. However, that sinner must yield to Christ for salvation, before Satan is obliged to release his victim.

The sinner, at his Cross-death, was completely changed. The body died, as the soul was taken out. The soul was put in Christ. Then Christ entered the body. This left no place for the evil spirit, so he just hangs around, looking at the house, wherein he once lived.

The best that the evil spirit can now do is "bewitch" his former house of mud. Although he is gone out of this house, he can now do a most uncanny thing upon the mind. He can think through the mind of the one he once indwelt. Bewitchment has to do with the thinking processes, does it not?

These Galatian Christians were being bewitched of the devil. The Apostle Paul called them foolish for allowing themselves to be duped into believing false things were true, at the same time disbelieving the Truth. Today, Satan, or any of his host, may cause the unwary Christian to disbelieve the truth of being dead to sin; The evil one may so cloud or darken the mind as to hide this glorious truth. Don't allow the Devil to pull a window shade down over your mind! An evil spirit may also place an imitation desire for old habits upon the mind of the converted one. This is wrestling the principalities and powers of darkness.

Satan Versus Christianity; Christ Self or Satan Self

A victory was won at Calvary. Whosoever will may share in that victory, by receiving Christ. This is salvation from the penalty of sin. There must, also, be salvation from the power of sin. There is! The victory over the penalty and power of sin was won at Calvary. Calvary must be applied in both cases. Before salvation, Satan dwelt within. God entreated from without. Now God dwells within, and Satan tempts from without.

When Your Name is Placed Upon Your Tombstone; Where Will You Be?

We must never imagine the Main Thing is going on right here. When your family is selecting your casket, where will you be? Oh, you say, I'll be down at the Undertakers. No! I'm sorry to contradict you; but, Unsaved Friend; you will have changed your address. Death is the moving out of the soul-man.

If one has harkened to his own thoughts instead of the Bible's teachings, doubtless he has been duped of the Devil. To spend eternity in a Hell that has been prepared for the Devil and his angels; when one might have, with much less effort nave accepted Christ, to thus dwell-in Heaven for ever, is nothing short of self-inflicted torment. No lost soul in Hell will ever be able to say, I once humbled myself and accepted the Christ.

A special place had to be prepared in the Universe to house the disembodied soul. The soul without the body is a ghost. This unclothed ghost must bellow hysterically in this City of Ghosts, O! How awful! I was Devil-deceived. I was brought here by thoughts of Christ rejection. I had thoughts on my mind, which were not my own. I am a fool! Here the time is, now F-O-R-EV-E-R!

History Solves the Mystery of Calvary; Calvary Solves the Mystery of History

His-story (history) will one day prove God started counting time when Adam fell. All this time will have been spent to un-do what Adam did-do. The lost man will learn in the first five minutes in Hell, that which he refused to learn during his entire life time. The first and greatest lesson learned there, will be what Eve learned when she harkened to Satan and partook of that "get smart opiate". What was that lesson? This costly lesson must be learned this side of the pit and death, or in the pit itself. What is that lesson? Satan deceives!!!

Christ Can Credit His Cross-Death to One Only Once

This cross-death can happen but once; hence one may be saved but once. Christ can credit, to your heavenly account, His perfection but once. The Eternal Spirit cannot sin. Therefore the one who is thus clothed upon could never be lost. If one is saved, is he not safe forever? If he is not safe, then it follows he is not saved. If salvation depends upon one's own righteousness, he could never be safe, thence, could never be saved.

Visa To the Upper-World

Wicked hands crucified God's Son, "Whom God hath raised up, having loosed the pains of death: because it was not possible that He should be holden of it" (Acts 2:24). A born again spirit, clothed with Christ, can one day step through grave clothes, walls, time, space, fire, distance, death, grave and flesh. Hell itself could never hold the born again spirit, who is clothed with Christ. Praise be to God! But! Oh! The agony of an eternal soul, crying out from somewhere in eternity, "I was converted too late!

Study, Discussion & Application Points for Chapters 8 and 9

1. Read and Study this chapter.
2. The key verse for this chapter is Romans 6:6: *Knowing this, that our old man is crucified with him, that the body of sin might be destroyed, that henceforth we should not serve sin.*

3. Great spiritual battles are fought in the minds of people. Scripture points this out very clearly. Note these passages and write down your thoughts:
   - 2 Corinthians 4:4
   - 2 Corinthians 11:1-3
   - 2 Corinthians 10:4-5
   - Galatians 3:1

4. It seems Christians should be very careful in controlling their thoughts. Ephesians 6:12 identifies our enemy, who operates in a spiritual realm. Note the instruction of the following passages and write down your thoughts:
   - Colossians 2:6-7
   - Romans 8:10-13
   - 1 Corinthians 15:57
   - Romans 12:1-2
   - Hebrews 12:1-2
   - Ephesians 3:16-21

5. We have learned that our "old man" has been crucified with Christ. Yet we still struggle with sin. The Apostle Paul described our dilemma in Romans 7:14-21. Notes these verses and write down your thoughts:
   - 1 John 4:4
   - 1 John 5:18
   - Romans 6:11-13
   - Romans 8:1-9

6. Dr. Lambert teaches us to "put to death" the old sin nature. Thus we are freed from the power of sin (see Romans 6:7 and 6:14). With this in mind, read Colossians 3:1-7 & 10 and write down your thoughts.

10

THE MYSTERY OF RIGHTEOUSNESS

That We May Present Every Man Perfect in Christ Jesus

Will you now permit the Holy Spirit to plunge you down deep into the water of the word? As great billows of joy unspeakable sweep over our poor heads, may we discover more precious truths; down in the depths of His ocean of love?

All right, may we then see what this is all about? Let us read a baffling statement, "We know that whosoever is born of God sinneth not; but he that is begotten of God keepeth himself, and that wicked one toucheth him not" (1 John 5:18). Let us add another baffler. "Whosoever is born of God doth not commit sin." Yes, we know full well the usual explanation: "The word commit means practice". But let us consider the rest of the verse which explains the first part, "For his seed remaineth in him and he cannot sin, because he is born of God" (1 John 3:9). This last part simply states: he cannot sin.

Why cannot the Christian sin? According to this verse, why is it that the one begotten of God, cannot sin? The answer is, "Because he is born of God". Well, bless the Lord! Certainly, this may not be according to our experience (for daily we have sin to confess), it may even be contrary to our best logic. But! Beloved, there it is, ''cannot sin!'' Believe it? We should! Because it is so! The Bible, without having any body's explanation says, "he cannot sin, because he is born of God".

Are we to believe that the Builder and Maker of the Bible allowed a serious error to enter in through the translator's pen? Are we not, rather, to have confidence in the Holy Spirit; the Superintendent of the Holy Scripture's construction; believing He did not permit blunders and errors to creep in?

The Spirit of God Bears the Spirit
The Spirit born of God cannot sin. "That which is born of the Spirit is Spirit" (John 3:6). That part of you which is born of God cannot sin. That part of you which was born of your earthly parents can do nothing but sin. But! That which is born of God is spirit; and that spirit part of you cannot sin. If it could even practice sin or sin without practicing it, it would be as big a sinner as the flesh.

His Seed Remaineth In You
However, let us not overlook our key which has been placed right there in the midst of the verse; within reach of all, "His seed remaineth in Him". Now, allow the Holy Spirit to interpret the word "seed" for us, "And to thy Seed, which is Christ" (Galatians 3:16). His Seed is Christ. "Christ in you, the hope of glory." He is our righteousness. His Holy Spirit fused with our born again spirit, has created a new man who cannot sin. Glory!

Many Scriptural Witnesses
May we now assemble many Scripture witnesses which will all testify to the same thing:

1. In the body of his flesh through death, to present you holy and unblameable and unreproveable in his sight (Colossians 1:22). Brother of mine, God is of holier eyes than to look upon sin; therefore, the Spirit means exactly what He says through the terminology, "holy, unblameable, and unreprovable". In Christ, you are thus presented to the Father.

2. "That we may present every man perfect" (where?) "in Christ Jesus:" (Colossians 1:28b).
3. Jesus Commanded, "Be ye therefore perfect even as your Father which is in Heaven is perfect" (Matthew 5:48). Note: Christ did not say, even as your Father is complete or mature. Be ye perfect! Could our holy God demand anything less than perfection? Could He, in keeping with His own holiness, command, "be ye fairly good?" Could our God require us to be ninety percent perfect, or ninety five percent perfect?

Yet, would our Savior, knowing the frailties of men, give us a command we could not obey? Yes, in grace, He would, and did. However, He does for us that which we cannot do for ourselves. By becoming one with us He becomes a very part of us. By becoming you with you, He can credit to your name in Heaven, His perfection. Thus, He commands, "be ye perfect".

This holy command causes us to search for other means than our own, in order to obey, be ye perfect. Certainly, this command compels us to believe that we need a Savior.

The law was Israel's school-master to teach them their need of Christ (Galatians 3:24). The law was God's Written Standard of perfection. Jesus was God's Living Example of One who had kept that law perfectly. The Israelite would measure himself by that law, and seeing himself a great sinner, would look forward to the Cross. There he would see his sins punished in Christ. There he would see himself in Christ, thus receiving Christ's righteousness as his own. Glory!

To Be as Perfect as the Father
The command, "be ye perfect, even as your Father in heaven is perfect", compels us to look unto Jesus Christ; who is as perfect as the One Father in Heaven, to give us His perfection. Thus we obey this holy directive.

A New Man Must Be Created As One Who Cannot Sin
In order to defeat Satan's plan to ruin all mankind; by causing perfect Adam to sin; a new man must be created who cannot sin. Although the

First-Adam creation did sin; the Last-Adam creation (new man) cannot sin. Does this not defeat Satan! May we put two Bible statements together?

> First – "That which is born of the Spirit is Spirit" (John 3:6).
> Second – "He cannot sin because he is born of God" (1 John 3:9).

Are not both verses speaking of the new birth? Are not both verses referring to the born again part of the new man?

"That which is born of the flesh is flesh" (John 3:6). We are compelled to agree with the Apostle, "For I know that in me (that is in my flesh) dwelleth no good thing" (Romans 7:18). Beloved, sin has to do with the flesh-body. In order to "present you perfect in Christ Jesus", (this side of the rapture) the sinful body of the flesh must be left here at physical death. Thus we will simply undress from these filthy garments of flesh and make our home going trip dressed up in the beautiful garment of His robe of righteousness. Praise God!

Death Permits the perfect born again spirit to enter God's holy presence

Certainly, the cause of death is sin. The point and purpose of physical death, from God's view point, is to permit the perfect spirit (born of God) to be freed from the body of sin. This permits our dear departed loved ones to enter into the presence chamber of our Sovereign God and Father; who receives His homecoming children. These saints are dressed up in Christ, who has clothed Himself upon them. Thus they are thus presented perfect. This may be verified by reading Colossians 1:28.

No Condemnation to Them Which Are in Christ Jesus

"The spirits of just men are made perfect" (Hebrews 12:23). "Now unto Him that is able to keep you from falling, and to present you faultless before the presence of His glory with exceeding joy" (Jude 34). "There

DR. J. PAUL LAMBERT

is therefore now no condemnation to them which are in Christ Jesus, who walk not after the flesh, but after the Spirit" (Romans 8:1).

If a man were short of perfection, he would be condemned, in Christ there is no condemnation, simply because he has a born again spirit which cannot sin, and he is then placed in Christ, where his life is hid with Christ in God. There, the evil one cannot touch him.

This is not Man Made Sinless Perfection
There is no such thing as a self-made-sinless man. The Bible does not teach the eradication of an evil root. "By the which will we are sanctified through the offering of the body of Jesus Christ once for all" (Hebrews 10:10). "For by one offering he hath perfected forever them that are sanctified" (Hebrews 10:14).

How are we perfected? By the offering of Jesus Christ. As God provided coats of skin for Adam and Eve, to cover their shame, so the Father permitted His Son to be slain in order that He, after His resurrection, might be clothed upon each sinner believer. Amen!

Sanctification, Not the Eradication of an Evil Root
One day "Gog", an atheist, is to sanctify God. Does God have an evil root that needs to be eradicated? Blasphemy! Thought be gone! God will one day be sanctified by Gog, the Russian Ruler of Ezekiel 38, when he makes his invasion of Palestine. Bible sanctification means set apart. Often times, mountains were sanctified, or set apart for holy purposes, vessels, in the temple, were sanctified, or set apart.

Christians are sanctified, or set apart, to spend eternity in Heaven, by the sacrifice of the body of Jesus Christ. All this can be verified by simply noting the Bible's usage of the word.

Jesus Dwells His Righteousness Within
Christ was not only our blessed substitute on the cross, but, praise be His forever, also, our righteousness in Heaven. "And that ye put on

the new man, which after God is created in righteousness and true holiness" (Ephesians 4:24).

There is no room for boasters or self-righteous folk in Heaven. "And be found in Him, not having mine own righteousness, which is of the law, but that which is through the faith of Christ, the righteousness which is of God by faith" (Philippians 3:9).

Christ in You
Truly, our hope of Heaven is in Christ's indwelling presence. Back on Calvary's Cross, Jesus looked unto you; saw you, fore-knew you, loved you, and knew you would one day accept Him. Knowing this, He took upon Himself your sin. Seeing that one day you would be in Him, and He in you; He would thus become one with you. Potentially, then, He became you back there.

Now, more than 1900 years later, the Spirit makes all that true by dwelling your Savior within your body. Before His crucifixion He prayed that He might be "all in in all". The Father answered that prayer. He struck out the time element, as Christ took your name; and in that sense became you back there. Today, He is a part of you; having become you with you. Thus He lives a perfect life in you, every day; crediting it to your account, as though you, yourself had thus lived.

What is Your Name?
Perhaps this next should be softly whispered into your heart. The first time you were born you became John Smith (or place your name here), the last time you were born, Christ became John Smith (place your name here) with you.

Jesus in His glorified body pays a visit to the Apostles in the Upper Room

"There is one body" (Ephesians 4:4). "And as they thus spake, Jesus himself stood in the midst of them, and saith unto them, Peace be unto you. But they were terrified and affrighted, and supposed that they had seen a spirit. And he said unto them, Why are ye troubled? And why do thoughts arise in your hearts? Behold my hands and my feet, that it is I myself: handle me, and see; for a spirit hath not flesh and bones, as ye see me have." (Luke 24:36-39).

The same flesh and bones body which died on the cruel cross; was buried in the dark tomb; is at that moment resurrected, and stands right there in their midst. His is now a miracle body; endowed with the capacity to admit and allow the habitation of each and every crucified believer.

Note these two verses: "If any man be in Christ…" "We are members of His body, of His flesh and bone" (See 2 Corinthians 5:17 and Ephesians 5:30). The risen Christ had just entered the room through the solid wall. His is now a Tran- solidi (pass through solids) glorified body. This tremendous demonstration was but one of a series of instructive lessons leading up to Pentecost. On that prophesied day, in this same upper room the Holy Ghost will appropriate to these believers, Christ's one baptism. That is, His crucifixion, burial, and resurrection. Each believer will be baptized, by the one Spirit, with Christ's Calvary Baptism; into that one body of "flesh and bones".

His One Body Has Now Been Made Omnipresent

"Christ in you, the hope of glory". Not only is Christ in you, and each believer; but, He clothes Himself upon each believer, including you. Jesus, in faith, prayed to His all wise and all powerful Father, asking that He might be glorified with this astonishingly terrific miracle of each one of His blood bought ones being in Him; but, He also prayed, "I in them". The same principle of glory (three persons in Christ), is to be bestowed upon those whom the Father gives Him.

"That they all may be one; as thou, Father, art in me, and I in thee, that they also may be one in us: that the world may believe that thou hast sent me. And the glory which thou gavest me I have given them; that they may be one, even as we are one: I in them, and thou in me, that they may be made perfect in one; and that the world may know that thou hast sent me, and hast loved them, as thou hast loved me" (John 17:21-23). By means of His Calvary baptism and His glorified one body, all this is to be accomplished. Each believer in Christ; and each one of these in Him. Christian, is this not glory!

Jesus in the Wall and the Wall in Him

As Jesus entered the room through the solid wall, He was for one short moment in the wall; while the wall was in Him. This demonstration in the Upper Room was a preview of what would transpire on the Day of Pentecost.

The Father Answered Jesus' Prayer on Pentecost

The Holy Spirit came on that day, and thus the Father answered His Son's prayer. He had prayed, "That they all may be one". He explained how this glorious miracle would be brought about, "As Thou, Father, art in me and I in Thee". Only Jesus, with His one faith could ask for and receive so great and so superior a miracle. The one hope is Christ in you. Even as He prayed, "that they also may be one in Us".

As several evil spirits, or even thousands, could be "one" in the body of the demon possessed man, so all of Christ's "born of the Spirit" spirits, can indwell Christ's One Body.

Cloven Tongues Like as of Fire

"Cloven tongues like as of fire... sat upon each of them" This was in answer to John the Baptist's prediction. Calvary was a public-historical event. It was the consummation of prophecies; and of centuries, yea, even eons of preparation. Pentecost was the public announcement that the Holy Spirit had come to bequeath and appropriate to each believer that which the blessed Savior has willed. Today, the moment a sinner accepts Christ, Calvary and Pentecost, and the eternal Inheritance is bestowed in one glorious package.

The Holy Ghost Wrote Through the Apostle

More than fifty years after Pentecost the Eternal Spirit wrote through the Apostle John, "And hereby we know that he abideth in us, by the Spirit which he hath given us" (1 John 3:24b).

11

THE SPIRIT FILLED LIFE

The Spirit Filled Life

"Be not drunk with wine... but be filled with the Spirit" (See Ephesians 5:18).

Perhaps these next words should be whispered; lest these soul mystifying truths shock your heart beyond measure. Pray that the dynamite of these indomitable words may blast loose every vestige of satanic influence.

When God, the Creator, brought Adam into being, He poured His breath-life into the first man. But! When He created you, a new creation, He poured Himself into you. What a thought! You, as separate and distinct a creation as Adam himself. You have all that Adam had, plus!

Fresh from the hands of God, Adam was perfect. Until the fall; Adam never sinned. The Christ-in-part of you never sinned; never will; because He cannot. "I in them, and Thou in Me, that they may be made perfect in one" (John 17:23).

How Does He Control the Believer?

Christ is just as real in you as He is on yonder throne. From that throne, in the glory world, He rules the universe. Sub-headquarters have been set up on the throne of your heart; in order that He may govern you. You must step back out of the flesh; back into the Spirit.

Here, Lord, you take over, please? I am unable to govern this flesh body. Should this not be the prayer-plea? Consider Calvary as an out an end to sin's reign. This victory was for you. It ended sin's reign over you. But! Satan continues to deceive you in this.

Sin's Conqueror abides within. You must step down off the driver's seat, and permit the Governor of the universe to direct. Eternal life in a time-born believer is gained when Christ enters in. Thus he becomes eternity-born!

Transformed
"But be ye transformed by the renewing of your mind" (Romans 12:2). This transformation immediately rouses and stimulates the thinking processes; the heart is energized by eternal motives, while the inner man displays exuberance for eternal things, as time and things lose their controlling power.

Present Your Bodies
Christ, not you, now owns your physical body, "For ye are not your own; for ye are bought with a price." He purchased for Himself the right to indwell and control that body. Beloved, you cannot walk, but He walks in you, you cannot lift your hand, but His hand is lifted with yours. "As God hath said, I will dwell in them and walk in them" (2 Corinthians 6:16).

There is One Faith. Not my faith; but His faith in me.
The Father answers prayer according to one's faith. Should not one, then, surrender his own poor little faith, and let it be supplanted by His one faith? God, seeing His faith in your heart, may grant that prayer accordingly. Jesus brings into your body His "cross death". When Satan sees Christ, instead of you, resisting his satanic force, he must immediately concede the victory.

The Abiding Righteous One Creates A Hunger and Thirst For Righteousness

Natural man has a natural hunger for natural things. Spirit-man has a hunger for supernatural things. Natural man seeks earthly wealth, fame, honor, and carnal pleasure. Christ creates in spirit-man a strong desire for heavenly treasurers; a holy reputation before Heaven. "For they that are after the flesh do mind the things of the flesh; but they that are after the Spirit the things of the Spirit" (Romans 8:5).

It's Not Your Life Now! Your Life Ended at Calvary.

Christ brings into your body His Calvary death. When allowed, He makes this real to the heart. He conquered death's reigning power. He conquered Sin's reigning power. By conquering death, He subdued its terror and power. He submits you to that death. Yet you, His own, continue to live. By the power of His resurrection over death, and by virtue of having subdued it, it is now gentle and docile. This converted death is applied to you the moment salvation becomes yours.

Remember, Dear One, Jesus removed the sting of death! "Know ye not, that so many of us as were baptized into Jesus Christ were baptized into his death" (Romans 6:3). His death was a death of terror and agony. But! He subdued it, He tamed it; it is now docile. He taught it not to hurt His own. "Knowing this, that our old man is crucified with him, that the body of sin might be destroyed, that henceforth we should not serve sin" (Romans 6:6).

You doubtless were unaware of the fact of that crucifixion-death. Although crucifixion death is the most terrorizing and the most excruciating of all deaths, you did not suffer. You hardly felt it. It was as gentle as an evening zephyr. You had to be told about your death, in order that you might know about it.

Consider the Trophies of that Victory

First, consider your death to sin! "For sin shall not have dominion over you." "For he that is dead is freed from sin." "How shall we, that are dead to sin, live any longer therein?" (See Romans 6:14, 7 and 2).

Second, Consider His presence, and the joy of it. Remember how you proposed to your darling? You wanted her! You wanted her presence. You desired to abide with her. "Now if we be dead with Christ, we believe that we shall also live with him" (Romans 6:8).

One Does Not Sin in Heaven

Our Dear Loved Ones, over there, see Him face to face. None the less' we may, down here, enjoy every other sense of His presence. We feel His abiding presence. We sense His nearness, as He hugs us on the inside! His love for us is keenly felt in our hearts. His loving heart beats for us, within our own. By this He sustains our life. He is our Life!

The reason our loved ones, in glory, have ceased from sin, is because they are dead. They are no longer in their sin bodies. Now consider; Are not you also dead? Does not your matchless Savior tell you, "But ye are not in the flesh". Then adds quickly: "but in the Spirit. And if Christ be in you, the body is dead" (See Romans 8:9-10).

Water Baptism is a Picture of That Death

Since you were unaware of this death, by experience; your Father had a picture made of it. That picture: Water Baptism! It was a beautiful portrayal of your death with Christ Jesus. That was a real death; but it was only for an instant. Had Jesus, your Lord, not conquered it, it would have remanded your body to the grave; until the resurrection. However, your Lord required your body, which He, Himself, might dwell in it for a season. By the power of His faith, yours is now a resurrected body. "But yield yourselves unto God, as those that are alive from the dead, and your members as instruments of righteousness unto God" (Romans 6:13b)

The End of the Temporal Life is the Beginning of Eternal Life

Death is the ceasing of one life and the entering into of another. Your Temporal Life ceased at Calvary. Eternal Life began instantly. This is death! You possessed temporal life; Christ possessed eternal life. "He who hath the Son, hath life (eternal life! See 1 John 5:12). Now that you are "one" with Him, you both possess eternal life!

Death means separation. Physical death is the separation of the soul from the body. That is precisely what happened at your cross-death. You, the soul, were taken out of the body, and placed in Christ's Eternal Spirit. "But ye are not in the flesh, but in the Spirit" (Romans 8:9). "For when we were (past tense) in the flesh", hence, "The body is dead" (See Romans 7:5).

Be Not Drunk with Wine

When one is drunk with wine he does not act like himself. When one is filled with the Spirit he does not act like his "old self". Christ dominates his life! Now, when the Devil casts evil thoughts and imaginations upon that one's mind, such as anger, bitterness, malice, envies, lusts, etc., the Holy Spirit captures them, and they are banished before they become sin.

If two people dwelt in the same body, which of the twain should rule? Would you not say, the one most capable? The One most Kingly! Should He not make all decisions? It is His body; He bought it, paid for it! You must not get in the way and hinder. Every day you must die to self.

The Portal To Life is a Tomb

We need not expect to live the spirit-realm life, unless we are willing to believe what a spirit is supposed to believe. The Portal into the spirit-realm is a Tomb! Your dear loved one died and was buried. You know that one still lives somewhere. Yet, you speak in this manner to others, "Oh, he is dead; he died a few weeks ago, but, I know he now lives in another realm." So, the Bible teaches that the believer is dead; although very much alive; just living in another realm. "And hath translated us into the Kingdom of His dear Son" (Colossians 1:13).

Where Does Christ Walk? On the Other Side of the Tomb!

"Walk in the Spirit, and ye shall not fulfill the lust of the flesh" (Galatians 5:16). Walk! Walk! But where? Walk in the Spirit! But where does the Spirit of Christ walk? He walks on the other side of the Tomb. Amen! Glory! Sin cannot reach you there.

"For he that is dead is freed from sin" (Romans 6:7). "Likewise reckon ye also yourselves to be dead indeed unto sin, but alive unto God through Jesus Christ our Lord" (Romans 6:11). This Devil staggering truth, when believed, deals his Satanic Majesty a reeling blow. The personal life of Christ flowing through the Christian's body and whole being; is a glory only born again ones may enjoy. These heavenly beings; left on earth to be used of their Lord. Amen!

The Two Sides to the Cross

There are two sides to the Cross. The Heaven side; and the Hell side! Two gangsters died; one on either side. One is in Heaven; one is in Hell. These two represent the whole Human Race. Which one represents you?

Study, Discussion & Application Points – Chapter 10 and 11

1. Read and Study these chapters.
2. The key verse for this chapter is 1 John 3:9: *Whosoever is born of God doth not commit sin; for his seed remaineth in him: and he cannot sin, because he is born of God.*
3. Dr. Lambert asserts the believer cannot sin because "His seed remains in us" (See Galatians 3:16). Of course the seed is the presence of Jesus Christ. Since Christ cannot sin, our new creation, composed of our new nature and the righteousness of Christ cannot sin either. Note these passages as a biblical foundation for this truth:
   - Colossians 1:21-22
   - Colossians 1:28

- Matthew 5:48
- Romans 8:1

4. Some teach that flawed human beings can reach a state of sinless perfection. Our practical experience clearly tells us this is impossible. How can we then rectify this truth with our practical experience? Read the following verses and note the word "sanctified". The sin offering of Jesus has provided a righteous garment for each and every believer.
   - Hebrews 10:10-14
   - Ephesians 4:24

5. An elderly man goes under the knife to have his foot and ankle amputated. He later gives testimony of what doctor's call "phantom pain". The severed nerves in his leg cannot quite justify to the brain the fact: the foot is gone. The man lies on his back and can stretch toes that are no longer there. He may scratch the stump and feel relief of a foot that has been done away with. Isn't it true that our old nature, amputated by Jesus Christ is gone and yet we can still scratch and flex the old nature (sin). However, in the midst of this our position in Christ has not changed and there is no condemnation (guilt).
   - Jude 24
   - 1 John 2:27-28
   - 2 Corinthians 5:17-21

12

TIME IS A PARENTHESIS
WITHIN ETERNITY

Our little time fretting clocks measure that portion of eternity allotted between the arrival and departure of one's life upon this terrestrial globe. Each tick of the time-piece simply announces another extension of the term of existence upon this earth. It guarantees not another extension. Soon this area of the Universe must recollect and absorb the dust part of one, as toll for the liberty of passing over Earth's Turnpike.

If the sin debt has not been paid, then Death, the toll-collector, must consign the soul to the toll-house. But God's debt paying Son purchased for Himself, at Calvary, the right to enter Death's realm and pay in full the sinner's toll-dues. This Wonderful Counselor Advocate assumes the obligation and liability, and pays in full the thing owed; when the sinner turns his case over to him.

This Attorney Has Never Lost a Case!
We, perhaps, cannot comprehend, with our finite minds, a thing as illimitable as eternity, But! I can grasp the length of one short month. Should you live fifty more years, Friend, only 600 months remain!

This Author deeply desires to meet the reader of this book, on the main Street of Heaven. It is hoped that many such appointments will thus be made through God. This may be done by accepting His Son.

Let us, dear reader, meet, say, over by the Fountain of the Water of Life. It is right over there by the Throne of God.

Will you not, even now, accept Jesus' death as payment in full for your sins? The Father has, already! The power of Christ's death destroys the power of sin. You can experience His death-power working within as temptation manifests itself. You may have both the death and life of Christ working in you. His death-life makes one free from both the penalty and power of Sin.

The marks of a crucified man are helplessness, utter dependence upon another!

In view of all that you have just read, a decision must now be made. One million millenniums from this moment, will you mournfully regret the decision, just made? Remember! Christ in you, the hope of Glory!

13

THE MYSTERY OF PRAYER

Pray Without Ceasing

Stupendous power is packaged in this word prayer. If its total potential energy were released, dead would spring to life, wars would cease, light and right would over-power wrong and darkness. A prayer may be powerful to the extent of the authority and force of the one behind it. Prayer is calling upon God to manifest His power and authority.

A prayer "authorized" of God, once brought worlds into being; suns sprang into existence, driving back the darkness; celestial bodies, inconceivably large and forged out of nothing, obediently began moving in their courses and thus a limitless universe was established. I speak of God's own dear Son. The totality of all power is His.

Doubtless, this next should be softly whispered into your heart, lest you be unduly startled by its terrific impact. This One, the Creator, dwelling within your body, may pray through your lips. Astonishing? Yes, but true! He, Himself so taught His followers to thus pray. Does He not abide within your temple? If so, why should He not be permitted to speak and pray through your lips? He, the Teacher, present within! Lord! Teach us to pray. The great requirement of this prayer is faith.

Believe the person of Christ, the Creator, to be as truly in you as you are in you. Should you allow Him to pray through your lips, rest assured that prayer will not go unanswered. No Word of God is void of power. A prayer may be powerful to the extent of the Authority and force of the One behind it.

The Mystery of Words

Words are the vehicles of thought. It is by means of words that earth beings communicate with one another. "I am fearfully and wonderfully made, that my soul knoweth right well" (Psalm 139:14). As the flesh is the visible manifestation of the invisible soul, so words are the audible manifestations of the soul's thoughts.

The soul, or inward man, has a wonderfully and fearfully constructed earth-house which has a built-in two-way audio-visual public address system, which is capable of the transmission and reception of thoughts, ideas, views, principles, loves, hates, grudges, like and dislikes, opinions, etc. These thought-messages are conveyed by means of powerful little things called words.

As a Man Thinketh; So Is He

Thoughts are the products of the thinking processes. If one is indwelt by God's Holy Son, His presence will be manifested by holy, righteous, and wholesome thoughts. God endorsed, in fact God-fabricated thoughts will be formed in the mind. Thus, the born again man is invested with a new character.

The Power of Words

May we employ our minds for a moment upon the consideration of the power of words, as spoken by any man? A word may be powerful to the extent of the power and authority of the one behind it.

Think of the power of the word "hate", as its evil comes forth from the lips of an enraged husband, addressing his broken hearted wife: "I hate you!" These words stir emotions of fear, frustration, great disappointment, and anger. All this may result in a broken home, separation, estrangement, divorce, and even murder.

Words set thoughts tumbling into the mind. Wrong words set wrong thoughts cascading into the heart. Wrong thoughts often produce wrong ideas. Wrong ideas may result in sinful acts. Evil imaginations are evil images seen by the mind. Many words are full of suggestion; some good, some bad. These stimulate the emotions, which in turn acts as an agent to produce vital activity which sets the physical body into motion.

Right words may produce right actions. Pleasant words have a tendency to stimulate pleasant and happy concepts. Well behaved words are a stimulus to good behavior. Immoral and naughty words are a goad to incite unholy conduct. One's deportment may be due to the conversation his auditory senses are in the habit of apprehending. Gospel messages, Bible lessons, and Christ centered conversation, have a powerful tendency to rouse the soul and spur it into right action.

"But every man is tempted, when he is drawn away of his own lust, and enticed. Then when lust hath conceived, it bringeth forth sin: and sin, when it is finished, bringeth forth death" (James 1:14-15). Thus we are admonished to have "The Mind of Christ". The careful consideration of these facts compels one to note the necessity of a full surrender to the indwelling Christ. Christ forms in our hearts the ideal. The ideal exists as a pattern of the perfect man He desires us to be. This concept, in our hearts, is there as a stimulus for our Christian life. Certainly we have a perfect Example residing within.

Scenes Portrayed in the Auditorium of the Heart
Evil Words may become vile pictures scanned in the theatre of the heart. On the stage of the heart appear many star performers, Lust, pride, anger, covetousness, reveling, idolatry, envy, and such like. Self is the main attraction, in every scene; and always receives top billing, on the self-applause meter. In behind the scenes, out of sight, always lurking in the shadows; is the production manager, Satan.

When the Lord Jesus takes His place in the Auditorium of the Heart, the scenes change with a new set of actors: praise, love, joy, peace, faith, goodness, and a company of others.

Words as Witnesses will Appear at the Judgment
"But I say unto you, that every idle word that men shall speak, they shall give account thereof in the day of judgment" (Matthew 12:36). Words, written and spoken, will appear at the Judgment, as witnesses to confront their author. Injurious and wicked words recorded on earthly scrolls will also appear again in the ponderous book of God Almighty! When time runs out, and the curtain runs down on the Final Act, then, for some, will appear these words: calamitous end!

Words of Fear and Disgust
Some words are verbal signals which cause the soul to recoil with fear or disgust: Such as war, filth, crime, hideous, destruction, threat, tempest, trouble, and a host of others.

Words of Authority
There are words of authority, such as: go, come, stop, proceed, etc. Consider the power of the word of one in authority, such as the President of the United States, or a dictator's word power. Christ spoke, and seas calmed themselves. Storms became docile. A minister speaks Bible words. These words set the power of the Gospel to working. This results in Heavenly family reunions. Oh! The mysterious power behind words! How can we even comprehend such power?

Words Reveal A Man's Character
Curse words (hell-language) reveal a man's attitude toward God. They cause God to damn, not the one being cursed, but the man cursing. Those lips should be praying, praising and entreating God, for a mansion in the sky.

Think upon the power of these negative words when spoken to God: "No, some other time. Let me alone. Some other time, I will not, etc..". Yet, consider the power of these affirmative words: "Yes, Lord! I will". Immediately a mansion in Heaven becomes the property of the one in whose heart these words are formed; in response to the Savior's invitation. This in turn produces the long sought for joy, peace, love, faith, longsuffering, gentleness, goodness, meekness, temperance.

Words are the raw materials out of which lives are made, in the factory of the heart. For in behind the power of words - are the forces of good, evil, right and wrong.

Words of Truth Create Power
Words are rendered powerful in accordance with the truth behind them. Here is a horrid word, "death"! Oh! The sorrow, the sleepless nights this tragic word brings when it is part of a message concerning a loved one. The truth behind the message, "sudden death" strikes sorrow into the tender hearts of the bereaved. Words of truth are the vehicles of power.

Terror should strike the unsaved heart, when it registers the word, "hell". The power of this dreadful word lies in the truth of its reality. We, who wonder on the edge of eternity and waiver on the brink of time are too fragile to completely understand. What an appalling thought! Fire-down-below! Accepting Christ as your Savior is the Hell-Shattering event of your life.

God's Words are Never Void of Power
"The words that I speak unto you, they are spirit, and they are life" (John 6:63). God speaks some mysterious words and angels come into being. Softly He utters a verbal signal and empty nothingness suddenly is filled with a mighty but intricate universe. Again He gives expression to two words, "Come forth!" And the dead is raised. Once He will shout and a moment later raptured millions will walk the streets of Glory. This is word-power - the power of the Word of God.

The Rational Principle Behind the Universe
"And the Word was made flesh, and dwelt among us…" (John 1:14b). As words are the vehicles of thought and power; so "Logos", The Word, is the personal manifestation of Deity: the actively expressed creative thought and will of God. "The Word" is a title of the Son of God. The Word was made flesh.

God's Written Word is the record of the personal word. The Bible then, is the written expression of the Living Word delivered with His authority and made effective by His power.

The Mystery of Prayer Words

As words are vehicles of power, so prayer serves as a vehicle of strength. Effective prayer, therefore, is a combination of power-words. The mystery of prayer, then, is the power behind it. But, what is the mystery of this power? Since prayer power is dependent upon the one behind the prayer words, then, would it not become a more effectively powerful prayer if the Living Word were the petitioner?

What a startling thought! A needy Christian praying to his Father, yet not he himself does the praying. But! Who, then, would be this entreated? Are you prepared, reader, for the prayer revolutionizing answer? "Christ in you, the hope of glory!" Amen! Has our loving heavenly Father furnished us, His children, with so great a provision as His Creator Son, our petitioner?

God's Front Yard

Enter into the night employing your back yard as an observatory; consider the magnitude of Earth's inky and star studded canopy. This immense expanse is but a tiny part of His vast universe. God's Heaven, beyond the "empty place in the sides of the north" must be a place of magnitude and glorious beauty, seeing that all this is but God's Front Yard.

Who is this that desires your full surrender? Is it not God's Creator Son? Dare you ask why your surrender is so important to Him? The Author and Owner of the Universe has fashioned Himself within your structure and from that position He longs to speak with His Father.

Lord Teach us to Pray

He must form that prayer on your lips! "Our Father which art in Heaven". In the light of the Mystery of the Ages, which is, Christ in you, to whom does the "our" refer? All the Christians about me, do you say? Doubtless, the Lord had this in mind also. But, down in the spiritual depths, will you not discover a rich jewel? A precious truth, one you will wish to embrace forever! I trust you will discover, for yourself, this truth, when I ask this question:

While in your prayer closet, as you shut out the world, everyone else excluded; for during this moment you desire to be alone: as you kneel; reverently, you wait for a short moment and you are quiet - listening! Breathlessly you listen. Harken! Are you not now, startled to learn: you, are not alone!

For some One's great heart beats within your own! Now, you may begin your prayer, "Our Father" (Jesus' and mine!). "Give *us* this day *our* daily bread. Will not the Father supply all His Son's needs, as He dwells in you? "Forgive *us our* sins." Does not your Savior identify Himself with you? Must He not assume the guilt of your sins and trespasses, before there is forgiveness? Did not our Savior die on the cross for these very sins, in order that He might pray to the Father in their behalf?

"For *we* also forgive every one that is indebted to *us*." Forgiving our enemies is now made pleasant, as we feel the dear Savior's compassion in our hearts for them. He loves them too, you know. He forgives them through our hearts. "Lead *us* not into temptation." Victory over every known sin is made possible by the abiding One. The Spirit of Christ catches the temptation as it enters the mind, and banishes it before it becomes sin.

Praise Him Brother, Praise Him!
"Deliver us from evil", "You have overcome them (the evil one and his host): because greater is He that is in you, than He that is in the world" (1 John 4:4).

Mystery of the Power of the Gospel
Is not this mystery of the Living Word, who speaks and prays through His own, substantiated by many other verses? Please consider the following: "Since ye seek a proof of Christ speaking in me..." (2

Corinthians 13:3a). "For it is God which worketh in you both to will and to do of his good pleasure" (Philippians 2:13). "Wherefore I give you to understand, that no man speaking by the Spirit of God…" (1 Corinthians 12:3a). "For it is not ye that speak, but the Spirit of your Father which speaketh in you." (Matthew 10:20).

Jesus gave a marvelous demonstration of full surrender to His indwelling Father, as God spoke through His Son's lips. He turned to His followers and said: "Verily, verily (definitely, positively), I say unto you, he that believeth on Me, the works that I do shall he do also" (John 14:12).

"If ye shall ask any thing in my name I will do it" (John 14:14). This is more than signing His name to your prayer check. Is this not Jesus Christ signing His own name as He prays through you? Glory!

"If ye then, being evil, know how to give good gifts unto your children: how much more shall your heavenly Father give the Holy Spirit to them that ask Him" (Luke 11:13). The Christian need not ask the Holy Spirit to "temple" Himself within because this is a very part of salvation itself. "Now if any man have not the Spirit of Christ, he is none of his." (Romans 8:9).

But! Should you pray the Father to give you the Holy Spirit to fill you, control you, and even pray through you, He will lead you to the place of complete surrender. Then you will step down from the driver's seat; step back into the Spirit to walk in Him.

The Holy One, now in control, will love through your heart; think through your mind; look out on a lost world through your eyes; speak and pray through your lips, and walk in your temple. Amen! You dedicate, He will consecrate! You deed-a-cate and abdicate; while He vindicates and consecrates!

The Gift of the Holy Spirit
"How much more shall your heavenly Father give the Holy Spirit to them that ask him?" (Luke 11:13b). Claim this promise; for it is God's! The Word of God may appear on this page - But! Behind that word! Remember! It is God's thought, once spoken - now repeated on paper.

A Flight Into Eternity

It is a short trip down the Isle of Life. But! At the end I see a door opened to a long new road - what a vista lays ahead! Amen! Is this The End?

There is no End!

Study, Discussion & Application Points – Chapter 12 and 13

1. Read and Study these chapters.
2. The key verse for this chapter is John 14:16-17: *And I will pray the Father, and he shall give you another Comforter, that he may abide with you for ever; Even the Spirit of truth; whom the world cannot receive, because it seeth him not, neither knoweth him: but ye know him; for he dwelleth with you, and shall be in you.*
3. The ongoing ministry of Jesus Christ overwhelms our feeble minds. He is sitting in majesty next to the Father; welcoming saints into heaven, building a place of eternal residence for every believer, indwelling the saints and praying to the Father on our behalf. Note these passages and after reflection, write down your thoughts:
   - Hebrews 7:24-27
   - Romans 8:31-34
4. How exciting to know that Jesus Christ prays for us. Jesus, who indwells us and is actually connected to our "new nature", seeks God on our behalf. The Holy Spirit also prays for all believers. Note these verses and write your reflections:
   - Romans 8:26-27
   - 1 Corinthians 2:10-13
5. Dr. Lambert points out there are words of authority. The power actually comes from the one speaking. Christ spoke and seas became calm! Words of truth create power and the words of God are never lacking for power. Effective praying brings a power beyond human understanding. Consider this truth

and then write down your reflections: Our loving Heavenly Father has furnished us, His children, with the wonderful provision of the indwelling Christ as our prayer partner and intercessor!

APPENDIX

Our Identity in Christ

It certainly makes a difference at how you view yourself. The inner "self-talk" of an individual will dictate their attitude, confidence, perception of those around them and more. Scripture hits this idea head on: *For as he thinketh in his heart, so is he...* (Proverbs 23:7a). Unfortunately, many believers look in their spiritual mirror and only see a defeated, losing, shameful Christian that has absolutely no power against devilish temptations and desires.

The Apostle Paul understood the power of spiritual "self-talk" and directed the Christians at Ephesus: *Speaking to yourselves in psalms and hymns and spiritual songs, singing and making melody in your heart to the Lord; Giving thanks always for all things unto God and the Father in the name of our Lord Jesus Christ* (Ephesians 5:19-20). Additionally, after rehearsing a list of spiritual truths, the Apostle urged the Philippians to *think on these things* (see Philippians 4:8). The result of this habit is found in the very next verse: *Those things, which ye have both learned, and received, and heard, and seen in me, do: and the God of peace shall be with you* (Philippians 4:9).

Satan will continuously attempt to deceive a believer into thinking they are unworthy, unforgiven, undeserving and forgotten. Scripture actually reveals that we are adopted into the family of God and our origin, purpose, identity and destiny are all determined by God.

Below are a list of scriptural truths that help define every believer. Careful reading, study and memorization of these verses can put a believer on solid footing when fighting doubts about our identity.

The Believer is loved by God
Herein is love, not that we loved God, but that he loved us, and sent his Son to be the propitiation for our sins. (1 John 4:10)

The Believer is complete in Christ!
And ye are complete in him, which is the head of all principality and power. (Colossians 2:10)

The Believer is God's Child!
For as many as are led by the Spirit of God, they are the sons of God. The Spirit itself beareth witness with our spirit, that we are the children of God. (Romans 8:14, 16)

The Believer is Christ's friend!
Henceforth I call you not servants; for the servant knoweth not what his lord doeth: but I have called you friends; for all things that I have heard of my Father I have made known unto you. (John 15:15)

The Believer has been made righteous!
For he hath made him to be sin for us, who knew no sin; that we might be made the righteousness of God in him. (2 Corinthians 5:21)

The Believer is completely forgiven of every sin!
As far as the east is from the west, so far hath he removed our transgressions from us. (Psalm 103:12)

The Believer is part of God's family!
Now therefore ye are no more strangers and foreigners, but fellow citizens with the saints, and of the household of God. (Ephesians 2:19)

The Believer has been made a new creature!
Therefore if any man be in Christ, he is a new creature: old things are passed away; behold, all things are become new. (2 Corinthians 5:17)

The Believer has been chosen by God!
Ye have not chosen me, but I have chosen you, and ordained you, that ye should go and bring forth fruit, and that your fruit should remain: that whatsoever ye shall ask of the Father in my name, he may give it you. (John 15:16)

The Believer has an inheritance awaiting me in heaven!
To an inheritance incorruptible, and undefiled, and that fadeth not away, reserved in heaven for you. (1 Peter 1:4)

The Believer has been given power over sin!
Knowing this, that our old man is crucified with him, that the body of sin might be destroyed, that henceforth we should not serve sin. (Romans 6:6)

ABOUT THE AUTHOR

Dr. J. Paul Lambert was an evangelist, revivalist, counselor, pastor, teacher and author that served our Lord faithfully for over six decades. Constantly in demand, he traveled to virtually every state in our country preaching in revival meetings and holding seminars and workshops.

He was born in rural Southeastern Kansas on February 12, 1906 and early in life became a printer. He married Emily Kite and eventually had three children: John Patrick, Joan and Judy.

It was during the Great Depression that Paul came to a saving knowledge of Jesus Christ and it completely and immediately changed his life. By his own words: "I knelt down a drunkard and stood to my feet as a forgiven saint in Christ".

Accepting a call to preach, he entered and graduated from the Kansas City Bible College (later to be known as Calvary Bible College). He pastored several churches notably The Church in the Country just outside of Bonner Springs, Kansas.

During the final days of combat in World War II, son Pat was killed on the Island of Okinawa. In the days to follow, God revealed much to Dr. Lambert and those truths became the foundation of his ministry and this book.

Following the war, and enduring for several decades, Dr. Lambert began a dynamic ministry as a revivalist and evangelist often preaching over 300 times a year. His communication style was dramatic, passionate and humorous. He became affectionately known as "Uncle Paul" to many of the people he ministered to. Careful records by our family verified over 100,000 souls coming to faith in Christ during the course of his ministry.

During his later years, he ministered in Kansas, Oklahoma and Maine. The last days of his ministry were lovingly directed to the Riverside Baptist Church in Hutchinson, Kansas. He stepped into heaven on June 12, 1995 to greet his Lord, rejoin his wife Emily, son Pat and grandson Roger. I'd like to think a long line of grateful believers soon formed to express their gratitude for his faithful preaching.

Both Joan (Mrs. Homer Quinlan) and Judy (Mrs. Ken Adrian) married preachers and together with their husbands enjoyed many years of fruitful ministry. Our family is very grateful God used Dr. Lambert in such a dynamic way. It remains a joy to know his impact continues.

God Bless,
Tim Adrian

Made in the USA
San Bernardino, CA
15 January 2017